HOW TO BEAT THE TAXMAN ALL YEAR ROUND

BRIAN COSTELLO

Stoddart

Published in 1991 by
Stoddart Publishing Co. Limited
34 Lesmill Road
Toronto, Canada
M3B 2T6

CANADIAN CATALOGUING IN PUBLICATION DATA

Costello, Brian
How to beat the taxman all year round

Rev. ed.
ISBN 0-7737-5483-0

1. Income tax – Canada – Deductions – Popular works.
2. Tax planning – Canada – Popular works.
I. Title.
HJ4661.C686 1992 343.7105'23 C91-095453-4

The author has researched all sources to ensure the accuracy and completeness of the information contained in this book. Nevertheless, we assume no responsibility for errors, inaccuracies, omissions, or any inconsistency herein. Readers should use their own judgment and/or consult a financial expert for specific applications to their individual situations.

COVER DESIGN: Falcom Communications and Design

Printed in Canada

Contents

Introduction

We've all seen changes from time to time, but, surely, the 20th century must be looked on as the time of most change — especially when it comes to tax planning. I mean, we've seen stock markets move to new record highs only to be massacred in October of 1987. We've seen investors make huge profits and suffer substantial losses. And then we've had the huge tax changes that seem to come almost monthly.

As if the tax system weren't confusing enough, the federal government and the provinces have introduced one tax change after another. They've made changes, rescinded them, and changed them once again. No wonder we find it confusing.

And now we have some tax reforms in place, but they have hardly simplified the chore of tax planning and filing our tax returns.

Lower tax rates don't by any stretch of the imagination suggest lower tax bills. The lost income-tax revenues will be recouped by increasing sales-tax revenues and governments' abilities to tax us in other ways.

As a result, it's up to us to learn as much about the tax system as we can. It's imperative that we take every tax deduction we can and defer taxes as long as possible and it's a must that we earn as many forms of tax-free income as we can. Here's the rationale: if there seems little doubt that tax rates are going to fall in coming years we should take every deduction we can get now when rates are still high. Even if we have to repay the taxes in coming years we will still be winners since we will repay them at lower rates than we save now. In addition, we can invest the tax savings and earn income that will give us even more money to pay our tax bills in the future. Naturally, we want to invest in safe, secure investments with good track records rather than risking our money by choosing investments that are more of a gamble than a sure thing.

I think How to Beat the Taxman All Year Round will be a very useful educational tool to help you understand the myriad tax changes, what you can do to protect yourself and how to use those changes to your advantage. As you read through the book you'll find there are many short chapters that each cover a specific topic. In addition, related topics have been grouped together in back-to-back chapters. The idea is to give you individual topics that you can study from time to time without requiring that you read the entire book in a sitting. If something whets your appetite you might go on, or you might take the time to seek out some professional help so you can implement some of the ideas that have been introduced to you.

Some of the ideas included in How To Beat The Taxman All Year Round involve the use of products like stocks, mutual funds, real estate and tax shelters. When you meet with a financial planner who sells these types of products you might suspect that he or she is biased, that he or she has an axe to grind because they earn a commission selling these products. Well, I don't sell products — in fact, I no longer take clients. I earn my living by writing books, articles, TV and radio shows and public speaking. As a result, I feel my research has made it possible for ordinary taxpayers to take these ideas to a financial consultant and know that the ideas can be implemented without worrying that they will be sold only product with no tax planning.

1

You Must File a Tax Return: It Could Mean a Rebate

Even though you have no taxable income, you may still find it worth your while to file a tax return. You may be able to claim tax losses that can be used to recoup taxes already paid in past years and you may be able to claim a refund for taxes already paid this year. It's the only way you can claim federal and provincial tax credits owing to you, and you must file a tax return and claim capital gains earned in 1991 — even though they are tax free until you exceed $100,000.

Many taxpayers who run a small business on the side while working full-time elsewhere make the mistake of comparing their income and expenses in the wrong manner. If their income exceeds their expenses, they claim it as a taxable income. If their expenses are greater than their income, they claim "zero." Instead, they should claim negative income equal to their losses. That will lower the taxes they were supposed to pay on their full-time income.

This same theory applies to self-employed individuals who have not earned enough to be taxable. It's important that they claim these expenses as they can be carried back to previous years' tax returns, which could result in a tax rebate of taxes already paid. Or these deductions can be carried ahead and used as tax deductions against income earned in coming years.

Rental income also falls into this category. If you have negative rental income it should be claimed on your tax return as it will save you taxes otherwise owing on other forms of income.

To receive the remainder of the child tax credit and qualify for the automatic advance payment next fall, the mother (father if he is a single parent) must file a tax return. Last November, an advance payment of $383 was automatically sent to those Revenue Canada felt qualified. To get the remainder, it is a must to file a return. Don't forget, also, that if you had a newborn in the last few days of the year you qualify for the child tax credit for that child for the entire year plus the full dependant exemption and one month's family allowance cheque. Everybody thinks that the first child of the new year gets lots of gifts, but children born right at the end of the year are worth cold, hard cash. One other thing to remember: even though the child born right at the end of the year didn't need child-care expenses, the family still qualifies for another $4,000 — provided, of course, that you paid child-care fees. If it cost $3,000 to care for one child you could only get tax relief for $2,000. With a second child you now qualify for $6,000 in tax relief, even though no money was expended on the second child.

It's also a must to file if you want to claim the federal sales tax credit. Every person who is 18 or over, is married or is the parent of a child, should look at Form T7078 to see if they qualify. Those age 18 and over must file a tax return to get it. Those under 18 will be claimed on their parents' tax returns. There is, however, a requirement that family income not exceed $15,000. Above that it is gradually reduced.

The interesting point is that a parent can claim a child over the age of 18 as a dependant exemption if he or she is attending school full time. The parent cannot claim the child as a $25 federal sales tax credit (FST), but dependants can *and should* file their own tax return to claim a $50 FST. The fact that they are 18 means they can claim their own FST. In fact, many families miss this credit in cases like this. They may not be able to claim their child as a dependant because he or she earned too much, and they may not bother with the FST section as their family income is well above the $15,000 level. In addition, the child may not be taxable because he or she didn't earn enough income. Yet, it's important that tax returns be filed to claim the FST in the dependant's name.

Another example involves individuals who married before turning 18. These taxpayers qualify for the full $50 FST, provided their spouse agrees not to claim this credit.

It's doubly important that taxpayers get accustomed to claiming tax credits that are rightfully theirs. As we work our way toward next year's tax return, when tax reform will introduce many more tax credits, you'll want to become more aware of how they work. Tax deductions lower our income for tax purposes. Tax credits wipe out taxes owing — and in many cases rebate to us taxes that we have already paid. The refundable tax credits give us money whether we owe taxes or not. The day is coming when it will only be tax credits. Get accustomed to it now.

2

File a Return on Time Even If You Don't Owe Tax

Many Canadians don't bother to file a tax return on time because they expect a tax rebate. They think penalties only accrue when they owe money and don't file on time.

Unfortunately, that's not quite true. You see, when the April 30 deadline rolls around, Revenue Canada instantly charges interest on overdue accounts but doesn't bother to pay interest on the money it owes us, unless the tax return has actually been filed.

Many taxpayers feel that they're earning interest on any rebates they qualify for even though they haven't filed their tax return, but such isn't the case. Revenue Canada's policy is that they'll start paying interest the day the return is filed or May 1, whichever comes later. That, in itself, is the perfect reason to get your tax return in early in the year when you know you have a rebate coming. Ottawa has already had your money for most of the year without paying interest on it, and they have no intention of starting to pay interest until May 1. Knowing that, it's advantageous to file as soon as you can. The sooner you get your rebate the sooner you'll be able to start earning interest on your money, or put it toward bills and credit card balances or your mortgage.

In fact, it's sad to say but many Canadians are caught in the trap of thinking that they have to pay their taxes automatically as requested by Revenue Canada and that they cannot get a tax rebate before April 30. Such is not the case. If you manufacture a tax deduction partway through the year that entitles you to a tax rebate or a reduction in your tax bill you can ask for an immediate tax change.

The other consideration that's important in this discussion is something called the three-year rule. It states that we can only go back three years when we want to reopen tax returns.

In 1991 new legislation was introduced into the House of Commons proposing to lengthen this rule to five years. Once it's passed into law we will be able to reopen another two years' returns. If you haven't filed a return for longer than five years there is no hope of recovering any tax rebates that may have been coming your way This change of rules allows those who have not filed in the past five years to get access to some money they could surely use.

The real lesson, though, is that you should always file a return every year. You save penalties and interest when you owe taxes. You get your money back plus interest when they owe you.

3

Why Wait for a Tax Rebate Cheque?

If we do one thing this year, only one, let's make sure we learn from a major mistake that many taxpayers are paying for right now. We fall into it every year so there's no better time than right now to make sure we no longer have this problem.

Many Canadians plan for their tax rebate cheques. They need this money right now to pay against their mortgages. After all, this is the time when many mortgages come due for renewal. Some taxpayers actually arrange for fewer tax deductions at source so they will get a bigger than normal tax rebate at this time each year. It may be for their mortgage, or a vacation or to send the children to camp.

When will taxpayers learn that there are better ways to put money away than to manufacture a tax rebate? Yes, interest is payable after April 30. But, don't forget that this rebate has been accumulating for months, maybe as long as a year and a half by the time you get it. The money is automatically deducted at source every time a paycheque is produced. Ottawa and the province have the money throughout the year without paying any interest. And, when they do get around to paying interest, guess what? It's taxable. That's right, while you are not able to pay your tax rebate against your mortgage and save years' worth of non-tax-deductible interest, you are earning interest from Revenue Canada that must be declared on your tax return next year.

The best thing we could possibly do is make sure we don't get a tax rebate. For about two-thirds of the population that sounds like financial suicide. It sounds like I'm recommending you increase your tax bills. That's not true. What I'm recommending is that you reduce the amount of money you *lend* Revenue Canada tax free throughout the year. Think of it this way.

Revenue Canada doesn't give back their money, they rebate our own money that we overpaid in the first place. Why not keep it for our own use? Don't let it be deducted in the first place.

The first thing you do is look at your finances. It wasn't long ago that you completed you tax return so you have a pretty fresh idea of what happened last year. If you didn't take advantage of any tax saving ideas and got a tax rebate it means too much is being deducted at source. Talk to the employment or accounting office at work, the local Revenue Canada office or a financial planner about how you can have the tax withheld at source reduced.

Maybe it would be wise to take advantage of some tax strategies right now. Most taxpayers are content to wait until the end of the year or the end of the registered retirement savings plan season. The rationale is that you don't get the tax rebate until you file your tax return anyway so why rush? Well, the answer is simple. If you learn the system you will find that you can contribute now *and* also get the tax relief right away.

If you contribute to your RRSP now, generally through a financial planner, you can request that the tax relief take effect immediately. You can, effectively, force your employer to reduce the withholding taxes that are remitted to Revenue Canada every pay.

When you contribute to your RRSP or any tax shelter ask the financial planner to provide an official tax receipt. You don't want confirmation of your contribution, you want confirmation of your tax relief. Take that receipt to your employer and ask that he or she reduce the withholding tax on your paycheque by the amount of tax savings. For example, if an average Canadian contributed $5,000 to his or her RRSP today he or she would qualify for a tax rebate of approximately $2,000. Rather than waiting until you get your tax rebate you would qualify for a reduction of about $50 per week in withholding taxes. In other words, your take-home pay would increase by about $50 per week. Personally, I'd rather have that money now than next spring.

It's best to ask the financial planner to complete the proper paperwork, have it sent to Revenue Canada, who will send back approval, and then take the approval to your employer.

You get another benefit as well. Rather than the $5,000, or whatever amount you choose, earning taxable income in your name, it will now earn tax-free income inside your RRSP.

This same strategy, by the way, can be used with other provable tax deductions such as alimony or support, business losses from previous years and tax deductions that accompany tax shelters. All can generally be used to reduce your withholding taxes. Use them now to increase your take-home pay or to reduce the quarterly installments you are obliged to make.

4

Being Late Can Cost You Money

We all know that our tax returns have to be filed by midnight, April 30. If we don't meet that deadline, we're going to have to pay some extra dough to the taxman. How much? Well, it all depends on how late you are. The sooner you get the return filed, the sooner you start to save money.

The first step should be to file on time even if your return is incomplete. If you don't get it in by midnight, April 30, you instantly face a penalty of 5% of the amount that you already owe. That's an automatic.

Then there's a second penalty equal to 1% per month to a maximum of 12 months.

And on top of that, you'll also be nicked with an interest bill starting May 1 until you pay up. The interest rate is changed from time to time as interest rates fluctuate, but at no time does it qualify as a tax-deductible expense.

Revenue Canada considers business and investment loans as tax deductible. But this loan is not. As a result, the interest you pay when you file late will burn a bigger hole in your pocket.

Even if you don't have all the information and even if you don't have the money, it's still best to file your return on time so that you can avoid all the penalties and interest that will accrue if you miss the deadline.

If you don't have the cash, Revenue Canada will bill you. And, yes, interest will be added. But at least you'll save all the penalties.

5

When It Comes to "Let's Make a Deal," Include Revenue Canada

Most of us are intimidated by the taxman, and justifiably so. We file a tax return that we feel is legitimate only to find out that it's not acceptable. But don't worry. Revenue Canada officials are always open to discussion, especially when there's a legitimate beef involved.

If you receive a request for more information, always reply quickly. The individual who looked at your return has the right to ask for clarifications. If you can't provide the information requested — or don't within a reasonable period of time — your tax deductions will be refused and you'll pay full tax.

If you don't have the right information, send in what you have. The assessor will look at it and decide whether or not to ask for more. If it's decided that your information is acceptable, you're off the hook. If you need more, you'll hear back.

In some cases, you may not be able to get the documents you need. The company may have closed its doors, you may be on bad terms with your previous employer, or you may not be able to find the documents you need.

If you simply ignore the tax department's requests, you leave yourself open to problems. They don't have the answers, so they can't be expected to make a decision.

When you get a request, give the tax assessor whatever information you can find. It shows that you are as interested in arriving at a settlement as the assessor is. As a result, you'll save taxes and penalties.

6

What to Do with Your Tax Rebate

They're coming fast and furious, by the millions. They can give us comfort and help to move us out of the recession — if we use them properly. What are they? Why, they are our tax rebates. Most taxpayers get one. But, not all of us use them properly. If we did we could manufacture some fabulous benefits.

Approximately three-quarters of those who file tax returns get a tax rebate cheque. That's a sad statement in itself as it shows that most Canadians pay too much tax in advance. Let's face facts, tax rebates are generally only the return of our own money. Had we enjoyed the use of that money all year we probably would be better off now than we are.

So, let's not waste any more time. Let's get those tax rebate cheques and put them to work.

Many taxpayers mistakenly believe that the money they have overpayed Revenue Canada earns them the same high interest rates that late payers are charged. That's not quite true. Revenue Canada does not start adding interest to our rebates until the end of April. Even then they won't start adding interest until we have actually filed our tax return. If you know Ottawa owes you a refund and you don't file, you won't earn any interest at all. And, if you do receive interest, it is taxable. Without question, you would be better off claiming your rebate as fast as possible and putting it to the best use possible.

Generally, the first thought should be toward paying down non-tax-deductible debt. We pay tax on the income we earn at work. We pay our interest with after-tax dollars. As a result, we could actually be paying the equivalent of twice the quoted interest rate.

As interest rates fall, we will earn less in savings accounts and term deposits. And, of course, that interest is taxable. As a result, we will be lucky to keep one or two percent of the quoted yield after subtracting taxes and inflation. Without question we will generally be better off if we pay those loans down.

The first choice would be to pay off our credit card loans. The interest rate is generally higher than the rate charged on any other type of loan. But, there's a second advantage. If you have a credit card balance you generally pay interest immediately on any new purchases until the entire balance is paid off. If you could eliminate your outstanding balance, new purchases would not accrue interest until your new date. It would be like getting an interest-free loan from your credit card company. If your tax rebate isn't enough to pay off your credit card balance try arranging a personal loan from the financial institution that issued you the card. Use it to pay off your credit card balance. The interest cost will be lower and you will enjoy an interest-free period.

Using your tax rebate to pay down your mortgage will pay dividends for years. Because these loans are amortized over such a long period of time you can win big in the future by using your rebate now. Each time you pay extra against your outstanding balance your monthly payment, which was based on the original balance, will become too large. It will now satisfy your interest needs plus leave a little extra left over to pay down the principal further. As a result, paying your tax rebate cheque against your mortgage can save many times over its value in future payments. It can actually shave years off the end of your mortgage.

If you are getting money back from Revenue Canada why not use it to save more tax? A natural use for your tax rebate cheque would be to increase your contribution to your registered retirement savings plan. The limits are higher this year so many Canadians will be able to contribute more. You can wait until the final deadline if you wish. By then, though, you will undoubtedly have already spent your rebate cheque. If you contribute it now you can ask your financial planner to arrange for an official tax receipt. It will prove to Revenue Canada and your employer that you have officially created a tax deduction. As a result, the withholding taxes on your salary can be reduced. Your take-home pay will be automatically increased each pay. See Tip 3 for more details.

We shouldn't restrict our tax rebate cheque to pure financial planning. Yes, it would be wise, given the prospect for an end to the recession, to invest it in stocks or mutual funds that will rise in value as the economy turns around. But, maybe you'd prefer to buy a new television or appliance. Maybe you'd like to put it toward a vacation, new clothes for the family, a gift for your spouse. Whatever, it pays to go after it and use it to better your lifestyle. But, don't forget to do your best to make sure not as much tax is withheld at source from now on so you will pay less tax this year, and as a result, get a smaller tax rebate next year.

7

Make Sure New Year's Falls on the Right Day

For individuals who work for an employer, they've no choice. Their year end comes at midnight, December 31, each year. For self-employed and businesspeople, though, it's a different story. They can pick and choose their year end — and save some taxes at the same time.

If you work for a company, you have to sort out all your financial affairs by the end of the year with the exception of one tax shelter, the registered retirement savings plan. As a businessperson, though, you can pick any day you want. For example, you could choose January 31 rather than December 31. When you do this, all of the income earned won't have to be claimed on your tax return until the end of the year in which you received it.

Having a company year running from January to the end of December means you pay tax in the spring when you file your tax return. Running from February until the end of January means the income wasn't earned by you until the end of next December and you don't have to claim it until the following spring.

Picking the right year end, then, can save you having to pay your tax bill for at least one full year.

Many individuals think this applies only to incorporated companies. However, such just isn't the case. In fact, it's often most useful to somebody who works full time at a company who also has a small unincorporated company operating on the side. The salary will be fully taxable while deferring tax on the unincorporated profits will give you working capital to help your company grow.

8

Start the New Year Off Right

So here we are, in a brand-new year — but this one promises to be more confusing than usual. We know the Conservatives now have a mandate to continue with tax reform and we know they have gone ahead with the GST. At the same time, we have confusion over the new registered retirement savings plan rules and the direction of interest rates. As a result, it's more important that we get the year started on the right foot.

The first thing to do is look at your investment-income situation. Remember, this is the fourth year of tax reform. Three years ago the $1,000 tax-free interest deduction was eliminated. The loss of this deduction hurts those who continue to opt for interest income. You'd be better off taxwise if you restructured your investments so as to minimize the amount of interest you earn. You could switch to blue-chip stocks that don't react with much volatility but that pay a good dividend and have for many years. Canadian dividends qualify for the dividend tax credit, which minimizes or can even wipe out the tax payable on these dividends.

Another consideration would be to buy some investments that pay a very low taxable yield right now but, based on past performance, can normally be expected to also produce a nice fat tax-free capital gain sometime in the future.

The easiest way to address this problem — and probably the easiest and least risky — is to contribute to your registered retirement savings plan right away for this year and last year. Most of us wait until the final deadline at the end of February to contribute for last year. But if you have the money in the bank earning taxable interest you're better off contributing now. The money will earn at least as much inside the plan as outside but it will compound tax free for as long as you leave it in there. The next step of course would be to contribute this year's maximum as well. Now you have two years' worth of contributions earning tax-free income rather than taxable income.

There's a very big change that will have a major impact on investors and the investment community. Tax shelters used to lump all kinds of tax relief into a year or two right at the start of the project. Now many of the tax deductions offered by tax shelters have to be amortized over five years. As a result, it is actually better to buy your tax shelters now, at the start of the year, rather than waiting until the last minute in December. In addition, the money you pay toward the tax shelter will no longer produce taxable interest in your bank account.

It is imperative that we look at investing in ourselves in 1992. That means pay off as many non-tax-deductible debts as possible. The natural start is our credit card balances. No matter how you look at them, they are a loan from the credit card company. In addition, they are, in most cases, the highest-cost loan we will incur. Credit card loans can cost as much as 28% interest when the compounding rate is considered. For those in the maximum tax bracket, this means the real out-of-pocket cost is more than 50% a year. That's a pretty good incentive to pay off these loans, wouldn't you say? All you have to do is to approach the card issuer and request a personal loan at 12% or so to pay off one that can cost as much as 28% annually before tax. Naturally, it would be even better to use existing cash balances to pay down these outstanding bills before you borrow.

The next step is to pay off other debts, including mortgages and personal loans. Non-tax-deductible debts should come first. Those bearing the highest interest are most important and those with the longest term of compounding should also be considered.

Probably one of the biggest mistakes made by taxpayers is to authorize their employer to withhold too much tax from their paycheques. Too many taxpayers claim they are single rather than married with a family. That way there is more tax withheld at source than necessary. Come tax rebate time, they get a nice, fat rebate cheque. But this is a mistake. If you really need a forced savings plan have the money withheld from your paycheque and paid into your RRSP or against your mortgage or other loans. That way you will save interest and also have a forced savings plan.

Other taxpayers have too much tax withheld because they don't claim tax deductions to which they are entitled. If you contribute to your RRSP or a tax shelter early in the year you have the right to petition Revenue Canada and have your withholding taxes reduced. After all, you are entitled to this tax relief. Why should you have to pay taxes on the amounts involved? In addition, if you pay maintenance or support to an estranged spouse and can prove it you also have the right to have your employer reduce the taxes withheld from your paycheque. For those who pay quarterly you can reduce your quarterly instalments by a similar amount.

Many Canadians chose not to cash in their Series 37 Canada Savings Bonds last year because they didn't want to pay tax on years of compounded interest. But now that we're into 1992, you should cash these bonds immediately and put the money to use elsewhere. The interest will be taxable in 1992 but you won't have to actually pay the tax until the spring of 1993.

One other strategy that will save taxes at this time of year is to contribute to a registered education savings plan (RESP). There's no tax deduction for your contribution, but all the money will compound inside the plan for as long as 21 years.

9

Don't Forget to Claim Any Extra Dependants that You Support

Under tax reform we no longer claim dependants as a tax deduction. Now they are a tax credit. That doesn't mean they are less valuable, though, since in some cases their value has been increased. The theory behind using tax credits is that everybody gets the same tax advantage. That means an increase in value for lower-income people and a decrease for those in the higher brackets. It also means that those in the mid to lower brackets should pay more attention to their relatives living in and outside Canada.

As long as an individual is related by blood, marriage or adoption, and lives with you, you may be able to claim him or her as a dependant exemption. Included are parents, children, grandparents, grandchildren, aunts, uncles, nieces, nephews, great-grandchildren, and illegitimate children.

Through marriage, husbands and wives, all in-laws, including brothers, sisters, grandchildren, aunts and uncles, grandchildren, nieces and nephews, great-grandchildren, and illegitimate children of a spouse can be claimed.

Those who can be claimed because of adoption include children, fathers or mothers, and brothers or sisters.

Remember, though, that there are also income restrictions. When filing your tax return, you should always check Schedule 6 if you have any dependants other than a spouse and children.

In addition, children, grandchildren and spouses who live outside Canada may be claimable.

And don't forget that single or separated taxpayers can use the equivalent to married exemption, which can save substantial tax dollars. There are also changes in that exemption, so make sure you check Tip 11 to see how it can help you.

10

You Don't Have to Be Married to Get Tax Exemptions

Parents know they get special tax exemptions for their offspring that can ease some of their tax burden. I use children in this example since a spouse is no longer an automatic deduction now that so many families have two working spouses.

And a spouse isn't even necessary when it comes to claiming dependant exemptions since single parents can just as easily claim dependants as can a couple. In fact, single parents can have it easier than the conventional family.

The first consideration is the equivalent to married exemption. It's covered in Tip 11. After that, though, there are other savings.

When two spouses are involved, the lower-income spouse must claim the child-care expenses. However, there are many cases where that spouse doesn't earn enough to be taxable. As a result, the child-care deduction is useless to families in that position.

With a single parent, though, there's less problem. In that case the parent involved has to use only his or her own income in arriving at child-care deductions. The same also applies to the refundable child tax credit. When two incomes are involved they must be combined to determine any restrictions. However, when there's only a single parent involved, it's more difficult to exceed the threshold level. As a result, the child tax credit can be larger for a single parent than for a married couple.

Single parents should also remember that day-care expenses can include summer camp, hockey school, etc. As a result, some of the expenses incurred in the summer months when the children are out of school can also be considered tax deductible.

11

Marriage Doesn't Always Pay

While marriage is a very strong institution, it appears that Revenue Canada is prepared to give more tax breaks to single taxpayers than to those who tie the knot.

For example: When a couple is married the higher-income spouse is now restricted when he or she tries to income split with the lower-income spouse through investment loans. However, when a couple lives together without marrying, there are no such restrictions.

Another case involves day-care deductions. With a married couple, the two incomes must be considered to see who gets the tax relief. Then it's the lower-income spouse who gets to claim. Effectively, unless both spouses work the family gets no tax relief for daycare.

A similar case can be made for the child tax credit. When two spouses are involved, their incomes must be combined to see whether or not the family exceeds the threshold level. Above that level their child tax credit is reduced. However, when couples live together they needn't combine incomes.

When a father and mother raise a child while living together without marrying, Revenue Canada now considers some of these tax deductions on a married basis. However, when couples live together without marrying and raise children by a former and different relationship, they get tax deductions as if they were single.

And don't forget to add in the equivalent to married exemption. It allows single, separated or divorced individuals to claim a child or another relative as a tax exemption equal in size to that reserved for a spouse. A single parent, then, can get the same relief as if he or she were married, provided a relative is being supported.

12

Family Problems Can Cost and Be Taxing

We live in a time when many families decide not to fight an uphill battle. They throw in the towel and move to two separate residences.

When that happens there can be some tax relief for maintenance or support payments made — but only if they are set up properly. Far too many families make private arrangements to handle these payments so that they can save some legal bills, but that can be a costly mistake. When it comes time to file a tax return and claim these expenses as tax deductions, they find that Revenue Canada has disallowed them.

The law states that alimony and maintenance payments can only be tax deductible if they are the result of a legally binding written agreement or a court order. Either normally requires some legal advice so why not see a lawyer in the first place?

You can sit down and iron out your own agreement without the help of a lawyer. But then you should take it to somebody in the legal profession to ensure that it's set up properly. The fees will be small this way. Rather than using a lawyer as a referee to arrive at an agreeable settlement, you can arrive at it yourself and use the lawyer to confirm it.

If you don't have a legally binding agreement, you'll find that Revenue Canada will deny the individual making the payments any tax relief and they may still find the recipient taxable. As a split family you don't want to share three ways; two is bad enough.

13

Always Let Lower-Income Spouse Keep Earnings

Recent federal budgets have done their best to eliminate income splitting, but they haven't been totally successful. In fact, there are quite a number of income-splitting techniques still available.

For example, you should do your best to let the family's savings grow in the lower-income spouse's name. That way the income earned by that spouse will be taxed at his or her lower tax rate rather than at the higher tax rate that may apply if it were left in the higher-income spouse's name.

One of the easiest ways to do that is for the higher-income spouse to pay all the family bills and all the lower-income spouse's bills. That includes his or her taxes, benefits, travelling costs, etc. That way the lower-income spouse will be left with his or her entire gross salary. It can be invested to produce income that's taxed at a low rate.

We used to give or lend money to a lower-income spouse to accomplish the same result, but Revenue Canada now frowns on those practices. This can accomplish just about as much good, though, when there are two working spouses.

Before tax reform we could each earn $1,000 in tax-free investment income. As a result, it wasn't as important to practice income splitting if we didn't earn any more than $1,000 through investing. Now that we can no longer earn any tax-free investment income it's even more important that we accumulate monies in the lower-income spouse's name. Let's face facts. If we have to pay tax we might as well pay it at the lowest rate possible.

14

Invest in the Lower-Income Spouse's Name

As I travel the country I'm regularly asked about how families should handle investments that are purchased jointly. The classic example involves sharing income earned in a joint account. Can we split it in any way that we find advantageous?

It would be nice if we could. Then we'd all claim the interest earned in these accounts in the lower-income spouse's name. Now that we can no longer claim the first $1,000 in interest as tax-free income, we could save some tax by claiming all the interest in the lower-income spouse's name. However, Revenue Canada is wise to that plan. They want us to claim the interest earned in joint accounts, and any other jointly held investments, for that matter, based on the amount of money each partner contributed. Technically speaking, you should compare your income to your spouse's and prorate the interest earned on that basis. If only one spouse works it's hard to believe that the other spouse could have earned any of the income generated by the joint account. However, if your spouse brought some money into the family from a previous job or an inheritance, let's say, it would be possible to argue that some of the interest earned in this joint account was taxable in his or her name. When one spouse has no income you must be careful when moving income to that spouse's name. While he or she can earn more than $6,100 income before becoming taxable, once the spouse earns more than $525 he or she will be eroded as a dependant tax credit. Effectively, the income above $525 will be taxed at the other spouse's tax rate, as he or she will lose a tax credit. But the higher the income the better off you are. Yes, you've lost your spouse as a tax credit, but he or she is taxed at a lower rate than you would be.

If both spouses work you would normally prorate the interest earned based on the difference between your salaries. However, it can be advantageous to do a little extra financial planning. If your spouse works he or she is probably lost as a tax credit. If he or she pays a lower tax rate than you, you should try to claim as much of the interest income as possible in that spouse's name. The tax burden will be lower.

You might be able to direct a higher percentage of the joint income to the lower-income spouse's name. Let's say the husband is the higher-taxed spouse. The family should try to use the husband's income first. That way they can justify leaving the wife's earnings in the joint account longer. Effectively, through proper bookkeeping, you will be able to show that the wife keeps and invest the bulk of her salary while the husband spends all or most of his. As a result, you should be able to argue that the bulk of the interest earned in a joint account belongs to, and should be taxed at, the lower-income spouse's rate.

Similar strategies can work with other investments as well. If you buy term deposits, try to justify them in the lower-income spouse's name. If you buy stocks and mutual funds, though, you should do an extra calculation first. When you earn dividends from Canadian sources you qualify for the dividend tax credit. Essentially, it's a rebate of the taxes already paid on these dividends by the corporation. If you have no tax to pay, this credit cannot be used. As a result, you should assess how much income your spouse will earn in the year to determine whether he or she will be taxable. If your spouse won't be taxable, it's better for the higher-income spouse to earn the dividends.

It's not unusual for spouses to jointly buy rental real estate properties. When you do you should be careful. If both spouses don't contribute, Revenue Canada will want all the taxes recorded in the higher-income spouse's name. If there are tax deductions involved it's a good idea anyway as there will be more tax relief generated. If you expect profits, though, you should try to justify some of these profits in the lower-income spouse's name.

If each spouse contributes the same amount to the purchase and maintenance of the building you should have no problem justifying joint ownership. As a result, you should prorate the profits based on how much each spouse contributes. This can be especially valuable when investing in something that offers capital gains, as it allows a family to earn $200,000 in tax-free capital gains rather than only $100,000.

If each spouse doesn't contribute cash it's still possible to justify some joint sharing. If one spouse contributes the cash the other spouse should handle all the work — the cleaning, management, renting and so forth. Then you can justify that the spouse contributed in effort and talent. All you have to do then is decide on a reasonable percentage of ownership for those services.

15

When Inheriting Money, Put It in the Right Person's Name

In most cases inherited money arrives tax free. It may have been taxed as part of the deceased's estate but generally arrives in the receiver's hand tax free. From then on, though, Revenue Canada hopes to extract its ounce of flesh as it will tax any investment income earned once the money is invested.

That's why it pays to receive any inheritances in the right person's name. For example, when a family inherits money it pays to split it evenly between both spouses where possible. That way one-half of the yield will be taxed in the lower-income spouse's name, if, in fact, it is taxable at all. Don't forget that even though we no longer have the $1,000 investment income deduction we can earn more than $6,100 in total income from any source before we are taxable. In addition, choosing investments that produce dividends, capital gains or rental income can allow us to earn substantially more before we are taxable. The dividend tax credit allows us to earn as much as $22,000 in tax-free Canadian dividends each year, the capital gains deduction allows us to earn as much as $100,000 tax free in a lifetime and rental income can be offset by the expenses associated with operating the building and capital-cost allowance when it is profitable.

The other consideration, of course, is long term. If one spouse is going to have a much better pension than the other, this type of tax planning can pay off in future years. Now that tax reform is going to eliminate pension rollovers to our registered retirement savings plans we know that our pension income is going to be fully taxable except for the pension income deduction. Arranging to have future investment income mature in the name of the spouse who has a small, or no, pension will mean that income will be taxed at a lower rate. Don't forget that when your spouse qualifies for the Old Age Security Pension that he or she will automatically be lost as a tax deduction. As a result, you should be doing your best to arrange your finances so income is generated in each spouse's name.

That's why it's important to take the time to sit down with a financial advisor, accountant or tax lawyer before you receive and utilize any inherited monies.

It may even be possible to put some of the money into your children's names where it can earn even more investment income tax free. Or you may want to aim for tax-free capital gains.

All of this, of course, may not be important. You may need the money to pay off your bills.

16

Let Everything Grow in Your Child's Name

Revenue Canada has done a pretty good job of restricting the practice of income splitting, but here's a way that you can still use it.

When we transfer money to a spouse's name or to a minor, the "attribution rule" says that we have to claim the income earned on these monies in our own names. So why bother transferring money to anybody else's name? Well, there's a very good reason.

It's true that income earned in this way is taxable in the donor's name. But if there's no income generated we don't have a problem, and according to the attribution rules, capital appreciation isn't considered income. That means transferring a pile of money to a child won't present any tax problems if the money earns only capital gains.

Realizing that, what if we transferred enough money to a child to buy a large piece of property on the outskirts of town? The property wouldn't produce much income unless it was rented out to a farmer — and even then there would be property taxes and other expenses that could be used to offset that income.

Between the time this property was purchased and the time when the property was sold, there would be a reasonable opportunity for it to rise in value. Generally, of course, that's what happens. Land on the outskirts of town rises in value as the town expands. In this case, though, the gain will be tax free or taxed at a lower rate in the child's name. This way the family saves on taxes.

17

Charging Your Child Room and Board May Save Taxes

Lots of parents have older children who still live at home. It's not unusual for them to charge room and board to those children. When they do, Revenue Canada takes the stance that the monies received aren't generally taxable. They aren't tax deductible for the child and not taxable for the parent as you're not really trying to make a profit. All you're doing is providing space in your home for family members.

In fact, to protect itself Revenue Canada doesn't allow family members to claim tax deductions in excess of revenues when they rent properties to other family members.

We can use this information to our advantage. Let's say you have some investments that produce taxable income. That is, you own interest-bearing investments, dividend-paying stocks or mutual funds or you've already claimed your $100,000 tax-free capital gains deduction. At the same time, you have a child who earns no income or very little. If you gave some money to that child he or she would be able to invest it and earn tax-free investment income. I know we can no longer earn $1,000 in tax-free investment income but if your children don't earn much income now all you'd have to do is give them enough principal so they wouldn't earn enough to make them taxable.

If, for example, you gave your child $10,000 he or she could invest it and earn $1,200 a year or more. That wouldn't be enough to make the child taxable and it probably wouldn't be enough to even eliminate the child as a dependant tax credit on your return. You've successfully practised income splitting. However, if you went one step further and charged your child $1,200 room and board you'd get back the $1,200 free of tax since room and board between families in this example is tax free.

This practice is easiest when the child is 18 or older. The child is an adult and can legally enter into these transactions. However, there are ways to accomplish the same or similar results with minors. If you have a trust in place it's easy. If you don't it will be more difficult.

18

Saving for Your Child's Education Can Save Taxes at the Same Time

If you have children, you may want to investigate the idea of a registered education savings plan rather than saving money in your own name. Money saved and invested by parents will produce taxable investment income. And that is sure to happen if you are to save up enough cash to send your children on to higher learning.

If you transfer money into a child's name there's no tax, but the income earned by that money will be taxed in the parent's name, not the child's. However, if you use an RESP — like Canadian Scholarship Trust Fund or University Scholarships of Canada — the money you contribute will accumulate in the child's name rather than your own. In fact, there's no tax at all until the money starts to come out in the child's name. By then, though, the money should have grown faster in a tax-free environment rather than in your own name. In addition, the money will come out of the plan taxed at the child's lower rate rather than your higher one. That is, of course, if the child is taxable at all. His or her income will be low at the time, plus there are the tuition and full-time student deductions to offset other income.

There are also other much more flexible registered education savings plans offered by stockbrokers and financial planners. They allow you to contribute $1,500 per child per year into one of these plans. Yes, there's no tax deduction when you contribute this money. But, all the earnings inside the plan compound totally free of tax for as long as 21 years. You are always guaranteed the right to remove the amount you originally contributed completely free of tax. The earnings will be removed in the child's name and taxed at his or her tax rate. Don't forget, though, that your children will have tuition, the full-time student deduction and their personal exemptions to offset or eliminate their tax bill.

With this type of RESP you have much more flexibility. You can put in as much or as little as you want, you can pick and choose the investment you use at any time you want and you can remove the money whenever you want. In fact, if your child decides not to attend college or university you can name another beneficiary — including yourself, just in case you want to go back to school sometime in the future.

19

You and Your Child Can Benefit from Borrowed Money

It's not often that we think about borrowing money for a child, but it can be a valuable exercise. We know our children have a regular income, and that's all they need to establish a line of credit. In addition, we know that they are generally debt free, so why shouldn't a banker lend them money?

The answer is that they're minors. They don't have the right to enter into a legal contract. However, if we borrowed the money for them they could service the interest cost with their regular income — their family allowance cheques.

That's right, the family allowance cheque belongs to the child. In fact, any investment income earned on money we give a child is taxed back in our own names, but investment income earned by investing the family allowance cheque is taxed in his or her own name.

The problem with the family allowance cheque is that it's a rather slow process to invest by the month. Instead, you could borrow $3,000 or so for the child and let the family allowance cheque pay off the loan each month. That way your child has a much larger pool of money invested right at the outset. That pool of money will grow faster than if you started out with a much smaller amount.

Because the child is a minor you'll have to put the money in your name. However, if you use the proper "paper trail" you'll be able to document that the loan was taken out for the child and the money invested for his or her benefit.

20

The Baby Bonus Is Really the Baby's

When the family allowance or baby bonus cheque arrives in the mail, it's meant for the use of the child. For some families that means buying clothes and other items the child can use. For others, there's room for investment.

Revenue Canada's policy is to have the parent who claims the child as a dependant also claim the baby bonus cheque as taxable income on his or her tax return. In the past, that was generally the father. However, with more two-income families it is no longer always the case. In fact, in a single-parent family it's pretty clear which spouse will claim the child and also pay tax on the baby bonus cheque. While it's impossible to avoid paying tax on this income — unless you aren't taxable — it is possible to use the baby bonus cheque to produce tax-free income.

For example: If you have the ability to put the money away for the child's future use you'll often find that you can't open a savings account for the child. Because the child is a minor, the institution will normally ask that the account be opened for the child in the mother's name. But that can create some very taxing problems. The institutions often send the T5 tax slip to the mother each year — and she often makes the mistake of adding it to her other investment income when she files her tax return.

Don't do that. You may end up paying tax on money that was actually earned by your child. Instead, claim it on the tax return of the individual who claims the child as a tax exemption. Simply claim this interest as net income of the child when you calculate the child exemption. That way it's earned tax free in the child's name and is allowed to compound for many years rather than being taxable on the mother or father's tax return.

21

New Year's Baby or Year-End Baby?

In the early hours of every January 1 members of one family in most cities are full of excitement. They are showered with gifts because their child was the first born in the year. However, those with children born just minutes earlier, before the year came to an end, should rejoice. They are the luckier ones taxwise. You see, Revenue Canada feels that December 31 of any year is the most important day of the year. What's in place at that time determines the amount of tax we pay for the entire year.

Those who give birth in the first few minutes of the year have their child for the entire year and enjoy the friendship and tax deductions that come with that child. Those who give birth in the last minute of the year only enjoy one minute of companionship but they qualify for every deduction available as if they had the child for the entire year.

The first deduction is the standard amount for dependant children. The first two children qualify as a $399 tax deduction as long as they were alive at the end of the year. Third and subsequent children qualify as $798 deductions. These deductions must be claimed on the higher-income spouse's tax return and can result in some sizable tax relief right near the end of each year.

The next advantage is the family allowance cheque, or baby bonus as it's called. This cheque is an automatic once Health and Welfare Canada knows about the child. If the child is born in the last minute of the year you still qualify as if the child were with you for the entire month. Those who give birth in the first minutes of January don't qualify until the next year.

The family allowance cheque is taxable income in the higher-income spouse's name and can actually be taxed away under the new clawback rules if your net income exceeds $50,850.

However, the child tax credit is not taxable income and can provide even more benefit for families who give birth right at year end.

The child tax credit is $575 for each qualifying child. Those born in 1984 and later can qualify for a supplement worth another $203. As a result, some families could receive a tax-free credit from the federal government of almost $800 because their delivery beat the midnight deadline. I use the word "could" as the child tax credit is "income sensitive." If the family's net income exceeds $24,769 this tax credit will be diminished.

The next consideration is child care. If we pay somebody to care for our children so we can earn income we can claim these expenses as child-care deductions. Children between the ages of 7 and 14 on December 31, 1990 qualify as $2,000 deductions if you actually spent the money. Those between newborn and age 6 qualify for $4,000 each in day-care deductions. As a result, a child born at one minute to midnight New Year's Eve can be worth up to $4,000 in day-care relief for the happy family. Yes, the family would not have had time to spend $4,000 on this child. But, that's not the way it works. If this family had another or several other children they may have spent more than $2,000 or $4,000 per child in day-care costs on them. The extra room provided by the newborn would make those expenses tax deductible even though they weren't actually incurred for the care of the newborn.

Child-care expenses can only be claimed when both spouses work, unless, of course, you are a single parent. They must have been incurred to allow you to earn income from employment or self-employment, to allow you to carry on research financed by a grant or to take an occupational training course where you get a training allowance. And, they must be claimed by the lower-income spouse.

When you start totalling the numbers you can see that they are definitely weighted in favor of having a child at year end rather than receiving a gift or two at the beginning of the year.

While the financial benefits are initially beneficial there is also a downside. There are age limits when it comes to social benefits. Once your child turns 14 he or she will no longer qualify as a child-care expense. However, he or she will qualify as an acceptable baby-sitter sooner and as a result may be able to eliminate the need for daycare expenditures. Other benefits can be affected similarly. And, in the very long term there may be an impact as well. By the end of the year in which a taxpayer turns 71 he or she must move the funds in a registered retirement savings plan into a RRIF or annuity. The individual born after midnight will have one extra year 71 years from now.

What's better? Some tax relief now or 71 years from now?

22

Use the Family Allowance to Buy Mutual Funds

Now that Michael Wilson's new budget plans to tax back the family allowance cheques from many taxpayers, it may seem that this cheque isn't worth a whole lot. However, there are a few ways we can make it grow rapidly. And we may even be able to get it to grow tax-free, or at least with very little tax.

First of all, there's no way we can avoid paying tax on the family allowance cheques. They must be claimed on the higher-income spouse's tax return when there are two parents. Single parents must also claim this income as taxable.

However, the income earned by this money can produce a tax windfall. If you earn interest this year from any source it's totally taxable now that the $1,000 tax-free interest deduction has been eliminated. But, as this cheque is meant for the child's use it's advantageous to deposit it into an account in the child's name. That way the income earned can be reported in the child's name and will normally be free of tax. But be careful. Most institutions demand that the account be opened in a parent's name in trust for the child. They then send the T5 slip to the parent. When these T5s are lumped together at tax time it's not unusual for a parent to add it to the investment income. That will make it taxable, as interest is no longer tax-free. Instead, this income should be claimed under the dependant's name on page 3 of the tax return. A child can earn more than $6,100 in income from all sources before he or she is taxable. For most children, then, this income would accumulate tax free.

It's possible that your child may be lost as a tax credit if he or she earns too much. However, because even at the best of times the child is worth only about $100 in tax credits, you are generally far ahead of the game by having this income earned tax free in the child's name rather than taxable in your own. With today's higher tax rates, surtaxes, super-surtaxes and the clawback of old age security and family allowance cheques, it's hard to find a case where it isn't better to earn as much income as possible in the child's name.

Savings accounts don't earn much. As soon as you have enough money saved in the child's account to upgrade to a Canada Savings Bond, term deposit or guaranteed investment certificate, you should do so.

In my mind, a preferred choice would be to use the monthly family allowance cheques as a forced savings plan to buy mutual funds. There's no question that they are considered long-term investments, but when children are young their money will be invested for many years and thus any negative economic factors influencing interest rates will be offset over time by more prosperous periods producing higher interest. Funds of good quality like Mackenzie Financial's Industrial Growth, United Accumulative, Trimark, Universal and a handful of other top-flight funds should produce an average yearly yield of 15% to 17%. That's far better than the 10% or less you can generally expect to earn with an interest-bearing investment.

You have two usual choices. One is to enroll in an automatic monthly purchase plan. The other is to save up a year's worth or more of family allowance cheques and buy funds once in a while. I prefer the monthly purchase plan. Because you are constantly buying, you get to take advantage of dollar cost averaging. That is, as the markets rise and fall you get a better average price.

There is a third option. It isn't used as often as it should be because most people don't understand it.

Here's how it works. You ask your banker to lend your child $3,000. It would be very unusual for the banker to agree because the child is a minor and cannot enter into a legal contract. However, it's not unreasonable for you to borrow the money for the child's use. But make sure all the paperwork spells out that it is really for the child. Now arrange for the banker to accept the monthly family allowance cheques to pay the interest on this loan. In fact, right now and as interest rates fall they should also pay off part of the principal.

Once you have the $3,000 you can buy top-flight mutual funds for the child. Based on past performance they should double in value every four to five years. If the child were age one when you started, there would be between $48,000 and $96,000 built up in the child's name by age 23. You may well lose the child as a tax credit and the child may even have to pay some taxes along the way; however, I have no doubt that the child is way ahead of his or her peers.

You see, what you've done is accelerate your child about eight years. That's about how long it would take for the child to accumulate $3,000 using the family allowance cheque. This way there's a much larger amount of money earning income sooner. In addition, part of the yield will be capital gains and part dividends so it will take longer until you or the child has a tax problem. It's a long-term plan. But in the long term it could work out wonderfully.

23

Winning a Scholarship Not Only Helps with Schooling — It Saves Taxes

Considering the cost of going to school, parents would love to see their children win a scholarship or bursary. It would help offset some of the expense. It can also mean a tax savings, in that tuition fees are tax deductible only in the children's names and not on the parents' tax returns. That means that any savings to the parents are the same as earning tax-free income.

Bursaries and scholarships can also be tax-free income for the children. In the first place, the first $500 is considered tax-free income. In addition, the student will qualify for the normal deductions and exemptions, plus the $10 per month full-time student tax credit. And tuition and moving expenses are tax deductible on the student's tax return.

Tuition is an easy one. It's always been tax deductible on the student's return. However, moving expenses provide the surprise. When a student moves home in the summer months, the travelling expenses are tax deductible against income earned in a summer job. But when a student moves back to school, the moving expenses are not tax deductible unless they are claimed against bursaries or scholarships. Once again, the winning of a bursary or scholarship has saved taxes as the first $500 is tax free and some or all of the rest is offset by the cost of getting back to school.

And don't think that a few hundred dollars worth of deductions isn't important! If you can lower the child's income far enough so that the student doesn't need to claim the $10 per month full-time student tax credit, it's transferable to a parent's tax return.

24

Why Not Get Paid to Look for a Job?

We've all heard of moving expenses, travel expenses, investment write-offs, and a myriad of others. But how many have ever claimed job-seeking expenses? The answer is very few. The reason, quite simply, is that few of us realize they exist.

If an employee spends money looking for a new job, he or she seldom gets any tax relief. However, if an employers spends money looking for new staff, he or she can indeed claim those expenses as tax deductions. So why not combine the two individuals to save a few tax dollars?

Spend your time and energy looking for that new job. Once your prospective boss is sold on hiring you, you probably have a little negotiating room. So why not ask for job relocation expenses? They could include the cost of moving you and your family closer to the new job — or they could simply cover your cost of looking for this new job.

Either way these are tax-deductible expenses for the employer. In the case of moving expenses, it's pretty cut and dried. With job relocation expenses, though, it's a little more complicated. Your boss will be committed to paying you a salary. It's a tax deduction, as would be moving or other expenses. Why not ask your employer to pay you moving or job search expenses, rather than salary, as these forms of income are tax free to you whereas straight salary would be taxable.

Actually, it makes very little difference to your employer. Both expenses are tax deductible so he or she doesn't pay a cent extra regardless of which way you receive the money.

25

If You Work Outside Canada, You May Get a Tax Credit

It's not unusual for major companies to transfer employees outside our borders from time to time. When that happens, it can open the doors to double taxation — in Canada and in the country where the employee works temporarily.

To offset this problem, Revenue Canada in some cases allows a special tax credit worth up to $80,000. In most cases that should be enough to solve this problem, and in many it might be a great way to earn some tax-free income.

To qualify, you must work in certain fields. Included are construction, agriculture, the exploration for oil, natural gas and minerals, and activities in the engineering field. If you're involved in any of these fields for a Canadian or Canadian-related company, and you work outside our borders, you should speak to your employer about these special tax credits.

In addition, these tax credits aren't limited to taxpayers who work outside the company permanently. If you spend most of the year working in another country you may still qualify on a proportionate basis. All you have to do is compare the number of days working outside the country to 365. If you worked two-thirds of the year outside the country, two-thirds of the maximum $80,000 tax credit would apply.

Before you jump for joy, though, talk to your employer to make sure your company, your job classification and your income qualify.

26

Stock Ownership Plans

Several recent developments paint a very obvious picture. Investing in equities will be far bigger in the 1990s than it was in the 1980s. In fact, it may become so big that it's commonplace, and considered the natural thing to do by most of us.

Ontario's New Democratic Party plans to introduce new legislation this fall that will give Ontario investors a tax credit if they invest in shares of small companies. In addition, they want to provide an even larger tax break for investors who invest in shares of the company where they work. Part of the rationale is that this would keep some companies from going broke and also increase productivity.

I have long been a fan of investing in the company where you work. In some cases key employees are able to arrange stock options. In other cases you buy simply because you work there every day and have a feel for what's going on. You know the company is profitable; you want to profit as it does. And, when you own shares you probably become just a little more productive.

I have also recommended that we buy shares for our children. As a longtime believer in ownership I think it's valuable to teach our children the theory at an early age. Buying shares in toy companies, airplane companies or the company where you work will have a special meaning for them.

Without question, this combination will encourage more people to invest in equities. That inducement will spill over into other companies and mutual funds.

There's something else, though. There's a group called the Canadian Shareholders Association in Windsor, Ontario. It encourages its 4,500 or so members to invest on a regular basis in things like stocks and mutual funds. The rationale is quite simple and proven to almost always work. It says that if you constantly buy the same amount of an investment over a long period of time that you will virtually always be a winner. It's called dollar cost averaging. Investors arrange for the same amount of money to be automatically removed from their savings account or deducted from their salaries each pay and invested in equity-based investments. Sooner or later they'll find they have a substantial pool of money and they didn't even miss the income.

The problem with this type of forced savings is that small plans get eaten up by fees. The CSA wants to implement a plan called Low Cost Investment Program similar to one already in place in the U.S. It piggybacks on a practice already offered by many companies.

If you enroll in this plan you will pick your stock holdings from a list of companies that offer dividend reinvestment programs. The association will buy one share of a company or companies for you. Once you own one share of any of these companies you have the right to buy more shares each year commission free. In some cases you can actually buy them at prices lower than the existing market price. Some companies restrict the amount you can buy to a small dollar value, while some let you buy as much as $40,000 a year. That can result in substantial commission savings and maybe a sizable reduction in investment cost.

Mutual funds have practised this theory for some time. They arrange to reinvest your dividends and profits each year so you have a much larger stash of money in the future.

The Ontario NDP proposal has merit. It's similar to programs already in place in Saskatchewan and British Columbia. Manitoba has proposed a similar idea. Quebec led the way with its OSSP and other provinces will surely look at this idea. In fact, it could eventually become a federal election platform since it provides tax relief at the same time as it encourages us to invest in small companies, particularly in the company where we work.

Here's the plan. Investors would receive a 20% tax credit on share purchases to a maximum of $3,500. That would provide a provincial tax rebate of $700. This wouldn't lower the cost of buying the shares but it would give you cash back when you filed your tax return to buy other investments, pay down your mortgage or contribute to your registered retirement savings plan.

The second idea is to encourage us to invest in our own company. We would be given a 20% tax credit on the first $3,500 invested, 30% thereafter to a maximum investment of $15,000. If the federal government joined in, the tax savings conceivably would double.

This is a good strategy. Right now we use deposit insurance to encourage savings. We'd be better off to encourage ownership. We'd grow as our company and the country grew. I hope other provinces and the feds get involved.

27

Having a Company Car Can Be a Taxing Ride

If you are supplied with a company car, you may have to add something called a standby fee to your income and pay tax on it. Revenue Canada feels that most employees who get company cars use them for both personal and business purposes.

If you, for example, drive your car more than 12,000 kilometres a year you can be nicked with a $2,400 taxable benefit on a $10,000 car. Depending on your tax bracket, you'll pay $100 a month or more to Revenue Canada for the right to drive this car.

Another option, if your employer will entertain it, is to have him or her lend you $10,000 interest free. You'll have to add $1,000 or so to your tax return for imputed interest (interest you saved by getting an interest-free loan as a taxable benefit). But you'd only have to pay about $500 in tax rather than $100 a month the standard way.

Of course, you'd also have to operate the car. To cover those costs you should arrange to bill your employer the going rate per kilometre. In most cases those expenses would be received tax free as they were incurred in the course of doing business.

There's one other consideration. You own the car, not your employer. As a result, you want to make sure that you save the tax savings and expense gains so you can accumulate enough to pay off the loan.

If you do that, you should end up owning the car in a few years. Eventually you'll be able to trade it in and start all over again. That is, if your boss is interested.

28

A Benefit Is Not Necessarily Taxable

Most of us don't get much in the way of tax relief when our employer gives us some extra benefits.

But what if you are forced to take something that you don't want? Well, that benefit may not be taxable after all. Revenue Canada is actually pretty fair. If you are a senior executive with a company that's worried about your well-being, so much so that they hire a bodyguard and provide a big black limousine to protect you, that won't always be treated as a taxable benefit. You should check with your employer or tax specialist to make sure that you don't pay tax when you don't have to.

Other examples include the obligation to put on major parties or suppers at your home. If the company reimburses you for the food and drinks you provide, or catering, there's not necessarily an obligation on your part to claim a taxable benefit.

In these examples Revenue Canada will look at whether you benefit or whether your employer benefits. For your sake, the answer will hopefully be that the company benefits more. That way it will get a tax deduction and you won't have a taxable benefit.

29

If Your Boss Dresses You, It Might Be an Untaxing Experience

Most taxpayers used to get some tax relief to help offset the cost of doing business. The rationale was to give employees a small tax break when they had to buy their own tools, safety shoes, uniforms, etc. It was called the employment expense deduction and offered a $500 a year automatic tax deduction. Unfortunately, Ottawa has eliminated that tax break as part of its tax reform plan. As a result, taxpayers who are considered full-time employees, that is, they are not classed as self-employed individuals, now get no tax relief at all for the cost of items they are forced to provide in their job pursuits.

Those who work at jobs where they have no obligation to provide special items were getting a gift so they shouldn't really object to the loss of this deduction. However, those who are obligated to provide certain items to get or keep their jobs are at a definite disadvantage. They now continue to make the expenditure but get no tax relief. Maybe, though, there is a way to get some tax relief.

Uniforms are a tax-deductible expense for an employer, so why not approach your boss about the possibility of having your uniforms supplied? That way you beat the loss of the employment expense deduction and may get a free uniform or two.

However, not every employer is prepared to pick up the tab for any extra costs. So why not try this idea instead? Ask your employer if he or she will pay the cost of the clothing if you'll take a pay cut of equal size. Your employer won't pay any more than originally planned and you'll get your clothes free and clear. The advantage to you, of course, is that initially you had to earn the money, pay tax on it, and then purchase the clothing with after-tax dollars. Now you get the clothes free and your tax bill is lower. In fact, if your employer has any purchasing power, he or she may be able to buy the uniforms in bulk at a discount. In that case your salary may well be reduced by only a small amount. You come out a winner in the long run.

The only fly in the ointment in this idea is the fear of losing long-term salary growth. Let's say you make an arrangement like this to lower your income by $500 a year. If your boss gives you a 10% salary increase next year you might come out $50 (10% of $500) short if your raise is based strictly on your salary.

Accordingly, it's important that you arrange for your employer to include this $500 as part of your salary when he or she gives you a raise each year.

30

Full-Time Workers May Still Be Classed as Students to Save Tax

Those who are full-time students qualify for extra tax relief that's designed to help them offset part of the high cost of attending school. Those who attend school full time qualify for the $10 per month full-time student tax credit — provided it's verified that they attend the required number of courses in designated institutions. Only institutions that offer courses beyond secondary school levels qualify though, unless it can be proven that the courses being taken are "trade" courses, and the institution is an approved one.

This is a very valuable tax credit in that it can either lower your own tax bill or lower somebody else's if you don't have any taxable income. As a result, every student should determine whether or not they qualify to use it — and I mean every student. You see, full-time employees may qualify to claim this tax credit.

A taxpayer who attended postsecondary school full time for part of the year and worked the rest of the year should claim for the number of months that he or she was attending school. That'll help offset some of the taxes owing as a result of his or her work-related income.

But, there's a way that we can use this deduction to save even more tax. If you work full time and take enough courses at the same time to be classed as a full-time student, you'll get the full $10 per month credit for every month you qualify. All you have to do is get the institution to confirm that you take enough courses to be classed as a full-time student and you've got it. In fact, when you think about it, many students who are taking post-graduate courses don't even have to attend classes. It's the workload that counts, not necessarily your attendance. Ottawa has also eased the requirements for full-time student recognition. As a result, it's now that much easier for full-time workers to also save taxes as full-time students.

31

Delay Accepting Income Whenever Possible

I know we want to earn as much money as possible, but there are times when we should consider refusing or at least delaying receipt of it.

Here's the classic example. It's late in the year and you're waiting for your production or sales bonus. You know it'll come very near the end of the year, and while it will be welcome you also realize that there's a slim chance you'll be able to spend it before the new year. If that's the case, why not ask your boss to delay it until the new year. Yes, you won't have access to it for a few more days or weeks, and yes, it's possible that you'll lose a little interest for that time period. But, don't forget that you also won't have to claim it as taxable income until next year — and you won't have to settle up with the taxman for another 14 months or so. Being able to invest the tax share for an extra 14 months will normally more than offset the loss of all the money for a few days or weeks.

When we work for an employer, he or she will normally withhold taxes from any earnings. As long as taxes are withheld on 70% of our earnings, we don't have to pay quarterly instalments on other income. We'll sort it out when we file our taxes. If you have other forms of income this planning can also pay dividends in another way. If you delay your bonus income until next year you may now be able to defer paying quarterly instalments on freelance income. Conversely, if you have not kept up to quarterly instalment requirements for this year, taking a bonus this year rather than next could save you having to pay some interest to Revenue Canada.

By the way, don't worry too much about your employer's reaction when you suggest some tax-planning consideration at bonus time. The company's year end probably doesn't come on December 31 anyway, so delaying your bonus for a couple of days won't cost the company any tax dollars. In fact, they'll have the use of the money for a longer period of time.

You will be a happier employee, and that's what every boss wants. You'll also be richer, and that's what every employee wants.

By the way, if your employer balks at this idea suggest that he or she look at using the same theory on his or her own bonuses. Then the reaction may be more positive.

32

Don't Pay Tax on Nontaxable Income

Tax reform is designed to eliminate many of the sophisticated tax deductions that high-income taxpayers use to save taxes. The trade-off, of course, has been to lower the tax rate we pay on our earned taxable income. As we lose exposure to making income nontaxable we may also be lulled into believing that all income is taxable. Such, fortunately, is not the case. In fact, there's a long list of tax-free types of income. Make sure that you aren't paying taxes on income that's tax free. If you have been, call your local Revenue Canada office regarding a reassessment. Income that's tax free includes:

- Lottery and gambling winnings
- War veterans' allowances
- Welfare payments
- Inheritances
- Veterans' disability and dependant pensioners' payments
- Spouses' allowances, but not alimony
- Workers' compensation payments
- Guaranteed income supplements
- Tax rebates, except interest
- Child tax credits
- Income earned by Indians on reservations
- Capital gains earned from 1985 on (to a maximum of $100,000 in a lifetime)
- Proceeds from sale of principal residence
- Live insurance proceeds on death
- Injury awards
- Board and lodging of employees at special work sites.

33

Make Money from Other People's Taxes

Everybody wants to make a little extra money. Some have more energy, more expertise than others. Some want to work part-time, others full-time. But to a person, everybody can use an idea or two. With the massive changes in taxes and the financial situation, there are jobs galore available. What are they? Read on.

If you're looking for a career change or just want to make a little money on the side, all the tax changes that are taking place and will in the future are sure to open up a few positions. Some will be full-time with government agencies. Some will be with accounting and financially related industries. Others will be part-time or entrepreneurial in nature. All mean lots of extra work for those who are looking. Ottawa couldn't get the provinces to agree on a combined federal/provincial sales tax scheme, so the feds went it alone. Instead of the existing provincial sales tax staff handling the federal tax, a whole new staff of thousands had to be hired. Those were full-time government jobs. However, a raft of part-time and freelance positions are available as well.

Large multimillion-dollar operations already have staff to handle the new paperwork. However, midsize companies, personal corporations and unincorporated small businesses are begging for bookkeeping help. There lies a fantastic opportunity. All you have to do is line up a small stable of clients and you have a nice seasonal job. Multimillion-dollar corporations have to file and remit monthly. However, smaller corporations respond quarterly or less frequently. They don't have a permanent staff. Accounting firms are swamped, so there are lots of opportunities.

There are courses on the GST much like the income-tax preparation courses. Those who can succeed pick and choose their workload.

This is the time of year income tax courses begin. With tax reform, surtaxes, the change to tax credits, constantly changing tax rules and a new tax return, it's almost impossible for the average taxpayer to complete his or her tax return. And it's going to get worse. There is a huge and growing industry out there that needs more part-time people.

The real advantage to this type of job is that it exists only a small part of the year. Individual taxpayers must file a tax return by the end of April each year. T4 and T5 slips aren't delivered until January and February, so you have a very short season when you can make a good living. The rest of the year can be free unless you decide to get into corporate returns.

The other advantage to this type of occupation is that it might become full-time. When you do tax return after tax return you see a lot of similar mistakes made year after year. Financial planning, without question, is the fastest growing industry in Canada. Building a substantial tax-return clientele may eventually inspire you to take more courses and enter the financial planning field.

Financial planning is not a part-time job. It requires a full-time commitment and constant education to keep abreast of changing times. It can, however, produce an income well above the average.

The economy has slowed down. When that happens it's not unusual for consumers to become a little slow in paying their bills. At the same time retailers are busy trying to control their inventories and promote sales. How about setting up a bill collection agency to help? We're not talking about a big, burly arm-twister. No, we're talking about a telephone service. Try approaching retailers and offer to telephone or write debtors asking for payment. Arrange to have all the cheques sent to you but made out to the retailer. He or she should be agreeable to paying you a 25% or so commission when you deliver the cheques. If the accounts are really overdue you might even be able to negotiate a better deal. And don't forget that you will now be a businessperson yourself. You will be able to claim your expenses as a tax deduction that will make it even easier to justify your business.

These are changing times. The Fraser Institute says the average Canadian pays approximately 53% of earnings in taxes. It appears that that percentage will increase in coming years. Add to it the complexity of tax returns and you can see why the tax field will present many job opportunities.

34

If You're Self-Employed, Don't Forget These Write-Offs

Revenue Canada has made substantial changes in the way self-employed taxpayers can claim automobile and office-in-the-home expenses. However, both (and many other legitimate expenses) remain deductible for those who are legitimately self-employed. It's imperative that every tax deduction is used to the fullest. After all, you know they will tax your income. If you incur expenses to earn that income, Revenue Canada should be prepared to pick up part of the cost in return for a partial share of the profits.

Following is a list of some of the out-of-pocket expenses you should not forget to use.

- Bank service charges and interest
- Couriers and delivery charges
- Entertainment and dinners for clients
- Accounting fees
- Advertising
- Business development expenses
- Office supplies
- Computer charges
- Car expenses, including gas, oil, maintenance, car washes, parking, insurance, licences, interest and depreciation
- Depreciation on any equipment purchased for business use
- Telephone charges
- Postage and mailing costs
- Salaries for employees whether full- or part-time, including spouse and children
- Office rental expenses or expenses (in some cases) even if the office is in your home

- Seminar fees when work related
- Two conventions each year
- Tips and coat checking
- Cab fares, airlines, limousines, parking, including meters
- Legal bills when needed to collect outstanding bills
- Cleaning bills when away from home
- Investment advice
- Subscriptions when business related
- Books and stationery
- Gifts etc., when given to clients, potential clients or as incentives to employees

35

Why Not Get Revenue Canada to Furnish Your Office?

Anybody who's self-employed realizes that office expenses are tax deductible. That includes rent, utilities, maintenance, etc., plus the cost of any equipment you may need. Large items like desks, typewriters, computers and so on aren't tax deductible all at once; they must be depreciated over a number of years. All the same, though, they do provide us with some tax savings.

But what if we buy antiques and antique-type furniture that will rise in value, even though we know we can depreciate them? We'll end up with tax deductions for the years we own them, and according to the new capital gains rules we'll be able to sell them totally free of tax as long as we're under the $100,000 maximum. In addition, if we really play our cards right, we'll borrow to buy office furnishings while we use our cash to pay off non-tax-deductible personal loans. That way the interest is also tax deductible — another tax deduction. It's a nice way to furnish an office, including antique desks and rugs, art and other artifacts at the same time as we get some tax breaks.

Here's the fly in the ointment, though. Corporations don't qualify for the tax-free capital gains holiday. That means that only those who run non-incorporated businesses qualify. But there are hundreds of thousands of self-employed Canadians who will. In addition, there are many employees who could encourage their bosses to buy antiques for their offices. The company gets the tax write-offs with the equipment being sold to the employees at book value or cost at a future date. It's an interesting perk, isn't it?

Revenue Canada is making it more difficult for taxpayers to claim an office in their residence as a tax deduction.

You must actually produce income while working in that office. Revenue Canada has long complained that a stockbroker, for example, did all his or her work at the company's office or on the road. There might be research done at home but that wasn't enough to justify tax relief. As a result, they now have put some teeth into the office-in-the-house regulations. To satisfy them we now have to see clients in this office or produce goods or services right there on the spot. In addition, we can only claim the expenses we incur against the income actually earned while operating this business. In other words, we cannot create tax deductions against other forms of income because our little "in-house" business was running at a loss. However, we can stockpile these office expenses and use them in future years to offset income earned when the business is more profitable.

36

Pay Up Early and Save Taxes at the Same Time

We all know that businesspeople get to claim their expenses as tax deductions. But when they pay them it can make a big difference taxwise.

Let's say you run a small unincorporated business or are self-employed. Your present vehicle is tax deductible but you've been thinking about buying a new one. What better time than right near the end of the year? Revenue Canada uses something called the half-year rule. That is, you only get to write off half the normal depreciation in the first year. But we're well past half year as the year winds down, so being able to get half the full-year tax deduction is actually a bonus.

As a result, it can pay to look at a new car or truck right near the end of the year. You get part of the depreciation allowable on your old vehicle plus one half the first year's depreciation on the new one. The older vehicle is probably worth very little as a tax deduction because you've been writing it down over a couple of years. The new one can create some substantial tax relief, though, even if you only bought it on New Year's Eve.

If you don't have the cash you can always borrow the money. The interest will be tax deductible if the vehicle qualifies as a business vehicle and so will the other closing costs.

The example we've used is a car or truck. However, those who qualify for tax deductions of this type could also benefit by buying computers, office equipment and other legitimate types of business equipment as the year comes to an end.

37

Does Buying a Year in Advance Save Taxes?

Businesspeople, whether incorporated or not, can use some equipment purchases as tax deductions. That's prompted some taxpayers to load up on everything they can just before the year ends so as to create extra tax deductions.

They would have purchased the goods early in the new year anyway, so they would have created a tax deduction at that time. As a result, it makes good sense to load up in advance. The tax break comes right away rather than at the end of next year.

Well, Revenue Canada has been catching on to this trick. They're not particularly pleased when you claim interest, rent, insurance and property taxes before their due date. So they may refuse to accept prepaid expenses in this category.

There are expenses, though, that should qualify. For example, if you buy some office stock that you know you'll use in the future, you have a pretty good chance. If you buy equipment at the end of the year that you can justify that you'll need early in the new year, or if you pay insurance premiums once a year rather than by the month, you probably have little problem in these cases.

Revenue Canada is fair. If you can justify the expense, they'll accept it. If you can't and if it looks like you're trying to beat them, they'll put a stop to it.

Whether you're self-employed or running a family business, you should seek out every tax break you can. It's better to claim a deduction and be refused than to have never claimed something that could have been accepted.

38

Don't Forget the Past and Future When Claiming Losses

Nobody wants to run a business at a loss, but in some cases it can be very beneficial not just for the present tax year but also for past year's tax returns and the future.

If you run an unincorporated business or share in a partnership that loses money in a year, be sure to claim those losses as a tax deduction against any other forms of income you had during the year. That includes pension, investment and other work-related income.

However, if the losses exceed your other forms of income, you don't have to stop there. You can carry them back and claim them against any of the last three year's incomes or forward for as long as seven years.

The advantage here is that you can pick and choose between as many as 10 years when deciding where you want tax relief. First, you should look at three years ago as next year you won't be able to include it. It'll be fours years ago by then. But don't let that be your only consideration. Your tax bill may have been substantially greater only two years ago, or last year for that matter. And even then you may feel that you will be in a substantially higher tax bracket in coming years. If that's your feeling, you may want to forget about the last three years and save these losses for future use.

By the way, you won't have any income. So make sure your spouse claims you as a dependant along with the children and also claims charitable contributions and other deductions.

When you look at this idea it's important to do some projections as to your future income. If you believe your income will be lower in future years you'd want to use up your tax deductions now when your rate is high. Conversely, if you believe your tax rate will be much higher down the road there is a case to be made for hanging onto these tax deductions for future use.

The other consideration is tax reform. There is a strong belief that when stage two of tax reform is implemented our top marginal tax brackets will fall. If you believe that, you'd want to use up your accumulated tax deductions before the lower tax rates were introduced.

39

You Can Hire a Family Member, but It's Easier to Employ a Friend

Self-employed individuals, or those who run a small business, can, if they wish, pay their spouse a salary. It's an excellent way to save taxes in that all of the family's income isn't earned in one spouse's name.

For example, an individual may run a small, unincorporated landscaping business. If the business is profitable, the operator will be able to claim operating expenses plus salaries and other deductions to offset that income. If his or her spouse is included in the salary picture, it's the same as income splitting. The profits will be less so there'll be less tax to pay. Part of the reason is that his or her spouse earned part of the profits and they were taxed at that taxpayer's lower rate.

Where this idea really pays off is when the small business doesn't make a profit — especially when it isn't an incorporated company — and when the operator runs it while working full time somewhere else. In that case, he or she can claim the losses as a tax deduction against the other forms of income, including a salary, investment income and pension. In this example, then, a highly taxed wage earner with few deductions can save taxes by opening a business on the side. By paying his or her spouse a salary, his or her normal tax bill will fall. At the same time, the spouse will earn an income but it will be taxed at a lower rate than the tax savings created in the first place.

In addition, salaries paid to children in the way create similar tax savings. In fact, though, it's even easier if you aren't married. Then you can pay a common-law spouse, let's say, in the same fashion. However, the restrictions that apply to setting up this business relationship are less restrictive when it involves somebody other than a spouse or a child.

40

How Would You Like a Tax-Deductible Vacation Every Year?

Self-employeds and commission types get a major break from Revenue Canada in that they get to write off the expense of attending two conventions each year if they want to.

Naturally, these conventions must meet certain criteria, such as having a direct connection to developing business or a better understanding of your business — and they can't be held in exotic locations like Hawaii with justification.

If the conventions meet Revenue Canada's guidelines, though, attending them can cut your vacation costs substantially. Let's say that you have a small landscaping company. The industry's annual convention is being held in Banff this year and you've never been to Western Canada. What better opportunity than to attend the conference where virtually all your expenses will be tax deductible? And better yet, if you stay over for an extra week most of your expenses for that week will also be tax deductible. Even though you aren't on business any longer your airfare or other transportation costs will still be tax deductible. The only out-of-pocket costs that won't be are food and lodging. In fact, they may still be a deduction if you can convince Revenue Canada that you were seeing suppliers or developing future business.

While you're on this trip, part of your spouse's expenses will also be covered. If you drive, there's no extra cost as it's only another seat in the car. And once you get to the hotel, it's only another person in the room that you had to pay for anyway.

Where you come out even further ahead is when your spouse works with you in your business. When that happens both of you are entitled to attend two conventions each year. That means you either get extra tax deductions for two conventions or each of you tags along with the other on four partially deductible trips each year. It's a super way to get in some travel and some tax relief at the same time.

Here's a further advantage that may help many individuals. If you work full time at your regular job, but have a small business on the side, you can qualify for the very same tax relief if you attend a convention or two each year. However, if your little venture doesn't always make a profit, these and any other business expenses can be carried forward and used to lower the tax you were going to pay on your ordinary income. You see, even those who aren't totally self-employed can get tax breaks this way.

Under tax reform, Revenue Canada will be more restrictive on the types of deductions we can claim when we entertain business associates. As a result, when we go on business trips or attend conventions, we must be careful to separate business expenses from food, entertainment and beverage expenses. Legitimate business expenses are still fully tax deductible. However, we are only allowed to claim 80% of our food, entertainment and beverage expenses when we file our tax returns. As a result, airline, train, bus, and auto expenses are still fully tax deductible, as are hotel bills, cabs, etc., but not meals, booze and a night out on the town.

This can be a problem at a convention. If you pay one fee that covers everything except out-of-pocket expenses you may not be able to claim the entire amount as a tax deduction. In fact, based on Revenue Canada comments, it looks like you will have to segregate $50 per day from your total bill and treat it as an entertainment expense. If there are no meals and no entertainment provided as part of the package you will have no problem with this calculation.

41

Make a Night Out Tax Deductible

Boy, the cost of living keeps right on rising, doesn't it? In fact, it's almost too expensive to eat at home.

However, if you're a businessperson, even if it's a small business that you run on the side, you get to write off all the expenses you incur to develop your business, even if it's down the road. So, why not time your business appointments with your stomach's demands? That way you'll eat at the same time as your business associate does — and the bill will be at least 80% tax deductible.

In fact, for salespeople or others who are compensated for their sales expenses, this is an even better deal. Revenue Canada demands only that the expenses be related to the development of future business — and that's usually easy to substantiate if you aren't cheating. All you have to do, then, is plan properly.

Here's who can really win, though, You have a landscaping talent so you start a business of your own using your garage or basement while you still work for somebody else full time. Occasionally you take somebody out for lunch or supper (it might even be a neighbor who you're trying to sell on your services). The bill now becomes tax deductible against the profits you're earning in this little business venture.

But what if you aren't profitable — which can easily happen with a young company. Well, in that case you get to carry your nonincorporated business losses ahead as a tax deduction against your other forms of income even though they aren't related to your landscaping business. Revenue Canada has long felt that this rule was an easy one to abuse. Businesspeople might claim a luncheon or supper as a business deduction even though it wasn't entirely business related. As a result, the rules have been altered slightly under tax reform. Now we can claim only 80% of meals, drinks and entertainment as a business expense. But even then, 80% is better than nothing. It still pays to arrange your affairs in the manner suggested above.

42

Travel Free and Get a Tax Deduction

When you travel on business, you incur some travel expenses. If you're self-employed, it's understandable that they will be tax deductible. But, when you are employed by somebody else, you should expect that person or company to reimburse you. When they do, you should be able to treat the funds as a tax-free reimbursement of business expenses. And why not? After all, that's all they were — your employer simply gave you back the expenses you incurred.

But what if your boss isn't generous enough to pick up the full tab even though you think it's justified? In that case you should claim that you haven't received a reasonable allowance to cover your out-of-pocket expenses. There's a good chance that you'll be able to add the expenses received to your income and claim them as taxable income. Then you'll be able to write off the expenses that you incurred as a tax deduction. The income received is offset by the expenses paid out so you don't pay tax on that amount — and the excess is claimable as a tax deduction against your income which should save you some tax dollars when you file your tax return.

Yes, it's better to have all your expenses picked up by the taxman. If that's not possible, any tax relief you can get is beneficial.

This tactic is generally available to sales types or to those who act as sales managers who are normally responsible for negotiating sales contracts. Those in different job classifications should seek professional advice to see if they qualify.

43

Donate Antiques to Your Favorite Charity

Tax reform has also affected the tax relief we receive when we share with the less fortunate. Those in the lower-income brackets actually benefit while those in the higher brackets don't receive as much tax relief. However, most of us may be able to manufacture more tax relief than normal by giving not money but something else.

Most of us give money from time to time to our favorite charity, but now that the tax rules have changed it might well be worth our while to give articles away that have appreciated in value. For example, if you have an antique that you purchased years ago at a low price, you could give it to your favorite charity at its present value.

You will have to give some thought to taxes, though, in that we're only allowed to earn $100,000 in tax-free capital gains in our lifetime. If you don't think you'll reach that point, you can get some extra tax relief without spending any money when you use this idea. If you think you will exceed $100,000 in your lifetime, you'll probably want to hang on to your antiques and give money or a life insurance policy to your church or favorite charity. See Tip 47.

If you purchased or inherited an antique years ago it's undoubtedly increased in value over the years. If you now donate it to your favorite charity you can claim a tax deduction for today's value even though it was worth much less when you actually received it. The increased value can be a tax-free capital gain, and any value above $250 will manufacture tax relief at the maximum tax rate regardless of your tax bracket. That's also a major change in that the first $250 worth of tax relief is at 17%

plus the percentage levied by your province. Beyond that you save 29% federal tax plus the provincial levy, regardless of how much money you earn. As a result, this tax tactic is as valuable to lower-income taxpayers as it is to those in the upper brackets.

44

It Can Make a Difference When Claiming Charitable Contributions

In the past we recommended that charitable contributions be claimed in the name of the higher-income spouse. That way the husband and wife would be able to claim the maximum tax relief regardless of which spouse made the contribution.

Under tax reform, though, we are going to change our attack. First off, it no longer really matters which spouse claims the tax deduction as we all now get the same tax relief. It's calculated as 17% of the first $250 contributed and 29% of the remainder. Those percentages, of course, are federal numbers. The provincial tax savings are added on top.

When I say it doesn't really make much difference who claims these deductions it's based on the fact that either spouse will create the same tax relief for the family. However, there are several other considerations. For example, taxpayers can claim no more than 20% of their net income in any year when claiming charitable contributions. If one spouse has a very low net income it may be easier to claim the charitable contributions in the other spouse's name. It seldom pays, though, to split them between spouses. You see, the sooner you exceed $250 the sooner you get to claim the 29% tax rate rather than only 17%. As a result, it's mostly a matter of deciding which spouse can claim the total amount of the charitable contribution.

There can be personal reasons for making this choice, though. It may be more advantageous if one spouse is, say, in the public eye, to have that spouse make the contributions and claim them as well.

It may also be advantageous for taxpayers to consider making charitable contributions in their children's names — especially when they attend postsecondary school. While a dependant's net income determines whether or not they can be claimed as a dependant tax credit, it's their taxable income that lets us transfer deductions from their names to ours. For example, if a student attending postsecondary school has no taxable income, he or she can transfer any unused tuition and full-time education deductions to a parent, spouse, or other supporting individual. In this case it may well pay for a parent or spouse to claim charitable deductions in the student's name so other deductions can be transferred to a higher-taxed individual's name.

45

Get Paid to Volunteer

Not everybody has the money to give to charities. People might like to, but they have enough trouble getting along on what they have coming in as it is. They might, though, be able to give their time and services to a charitable organization.

If you donate time, you normally cannot get a tax deduction. Revenue Canada feels that your time is worthless until you get paid for it. If you give it away, you're falling right into their hands — you get no tax deduction.

If you are a printer or manufacturer, you have a better chance in that you can, at least, recover your costs as a tax-deductible donation. In point of fact, though, there are occasions where charities have given receipts for work done on their behalf even though no money actually changed hands.

And many charities seem open to the following: if you incur expenses while doing volunteer work, try submitting those expenses to the charity. We're talking about gas, oil, parking, telephone calls, stationery, stamps, etc. They may not be open to outright paying for them, as you hope they will, but they may be prepared to issue a tax slip showing that you donated an equivalent amount of money to that charity.

At least you'll get back part of your money from the taxman.

This year, this tax tactic is more valuable than in the past. Remember, once we exceed $250 in charitable deductions we enjoy tax relief at the lofty rates used by those in the highest tax brackets. If you exceed $250 you will get back close to half of your out-of-pocket expenses. It means those with the time can more easily justify giving their time to worthwhile causes.

46

Use Political Donations Properly

While tax reform has dramatically changed the way we claim many of our tax deductions, it has not changed the way we benefit when we contribute to the political party of our choice. In fact, when you look closely you can see that many of the new tax calculations have been altered so they mimic the tax strategies we use when we claim political tax credits.

Even though majority governments mean that we only have elections every four or five years, political parties are always out to raise money. Their task has been made somewhat easier in recent years as we now qualify for substantial tax rebates when we contribute to our favorite political party. And I mean tax rebates, not just tax deductions. The advantage of tax rebates is that they mean just as much, maybe more, to the mid- and lower-income brackets as they do to those at the high-income levels.

For example, no matter how much income you earn or how much tax you pay, you'll get a tax rebate or reduction of $75 when you donate $100 to your favorite federal party.The next $450 that you contribute qualifies for a 50% tax break with any additional contributions worth 33 1/3 cents on the dollar until you reach a maximum tax credit of $500. Realizing this, it becomes fairly obvious how we can save a few extra tax dollars when we contribute money to a federal political party. If the husband gives $200 while the wife gives nothing, the family saves $125 in tax. However, if the husband gives $100 while the wife also gives $100, the family would save $150 in taxes, $25 more. Obviously, then, it pays to split political contributions between spouses. You'll save extra taxes.

47

Give Your Life Insurance Away

Lots of Canadians would like to give money to their church or favorite charity, but don't feel they can go as far as they wish. They just don't have the resources. Retirement time is coming soon and they're trying to amass as much money as they can as they know they'll have to supplement their pension income.

Life insurance may be the answer — not buying it, but giving away an existing policy. Most of us buy life insurance when we are young to provide protection for our families while we amass enough resources to take care of them. However, once we've paid for our houses and educated our children we don't need life insurance as much, especially when our health is reasonable good.

But rather than cancel the policy, maybe we could use it to get some tax relief. If the policy is a cash-value-type policy — that is, something other than term insurance — you could give the built-up value to your church or charity. The total built-up value would be tax deductible as a charitable donation, which would save you tax dollars, probably when your tax bracket is at its highest. The saved taxes would then be available to help supplement your pension income when you retire.

Your policy may have a paid-up value, which would mean you didn't have to make any further payments. However, if you did continue to pay monthly or yearly payments after giving this policy away, you'd be able to claim them as tax deductions as they'd also be helping out a charity or a church.

The charity or church won't be as disposed to this action as it would be to cash, but when you die and the organization gets a substantial sum of money it will be quite thankful.

When it comes to making this decision, don't forget about your family. If they're going to need the money for funeral bills and the like, make sure they come first.

Those in the higher tax brackets always found giving money or assets to charities more advantageous than did those in the lower brackets. The tax relief was always better. Under tax reform, though, the advantages are almost reversed.

From now on the tax relief on the first $250 is a tax reduction of 17% plus the additional provincial increase. As a result, everybody is treated the same. That suggests that lower-income taxpayers will get more tax advantage when they contribute than higher-income taxpayers did. Once you exceed $250, though, lower-income individuals do even better than higher-income earners. Regardless of your income, anybody who contributes more than $250 gets tax relief at the highest possible marginal rate regardless of their tax rate.

To narrow this down to the easiest understandable quotient here's what to do. Everybody should contribute to the charity of their choice. Those in the lower brackets get an extra bonus. Everybody gets the maximum tax deduction once they contribute more than $250. As a result, higher-income types should continue to contribute as they pay a small price in the way of a lower deduction on the first $250. Those in the lower brackets should escalate their contributions as they get much more tax relief than normal.

However, when it comes to choosing between an RRSP and a charitable contribution it pays to pick the former. You get tax relief plus you keep your money and it compounds for a lifetime.

48

Can't Afford a Home? This Way You Might Be Able To

While it's the great Canadian dream to own a house, it's not always possible because of the cost associated with owning property.

Oh, if we could only enjoy the advantages of being a homeowner in the United States. Americans can write off all their mortgage interest, plus in many cases the interest they pay on appliance and other purchase loans. Well, we might be able to as well.

Picture a new condo development in your municipality. If you buy a unit on the tenth floor for your own use, you get no tax relief. However, if you buy a unit and rent it out you can write off all of your expenses, including interest, taxes, maintenance, utilities, insurance and more. So, why not buy on the eleventh floor and rent it to somebody — and talk that person into buying the tenth-floor unit and renting it to you. You each get the unit you want and you each get a raft of tax relief because you own rental property.

While it sounds simple, it isn't quite. You will have to pay rent to the owner of your condo and you will have to collect rent from the renter of yours. But that shouldn't really pose a problem. And maintenance won't be a headache either as you're in the same building paying the same maintenance fees, plus you'll be able to keep an eye on each other's properties.

Five years, 10 years, who knows how long down the road, all you have to do is sell these properties to each other. You've enjoyed the tax advantages, and now you get to sell (and own) without paying any capital gains taxes.

49

When You Own Mortgages or Annuities, Don't Pay Extra Tax

I have a definite preference for investments other than those that are simply interest bearing. Interest is taxable, whereas dividends from Canadian investments qualify for the dividend tax credit, and capital gains are tax free to a maximum of $100,000 in a lifetime (farms and small business, $500,000).

In addition, some Canadians get lulled into paying more tax on some interest-bearing investments than need be.

When you lend somebody money through a mortgage, you normally amortize the loan over a long period of time. Using an amortization schedule, the borrower will pay the loan off in a series of equal monthly payments that are part interest and part principal. The interest portion is, indeed, taxable in your name, now that the $1,000 tax-free interest deduction has been cancelled. But, even before this tax change, the interest portion could have been taxable for many mortgage lenders. You see, if you lent money to a family member or a business associate it never qualified for the $1,000 tax-free deduction. And once you exceeded $1,000 the remainder was always taxable. But, *the principal portion of these payments is tax free*. After all, it's simply the return of your own money, so why should you pay any tax on it?

Make sure you get an amortization schedule that shows how much of the income you earn from a mortgage is taxable and how much isn't. That way you won't pay any more tax than is necessary.

A similar case exists when you have an annuity purchased with non-tax-sheltered cash. If you used funds inside your RRSP to purchase an annuity, all the income you earn is taxable. If you used Income Averaging Annuity Contracts to save taxes several years ago, the income you earn from these investments is totally taxable as well. However, if you used savings to purchase an annuity as a pension, you should pay tax on the interest only.

50

Renegotiating Your Loan

Can you imagine any time when we have had a better opportunity to make or save money than right now? Interest rates have fallen but millions of borrowers are still accepting high rates, even though they don't have to. *There is no obligation to automatically accept high interest rates.*

If none of your loans have come due for renewal you haven't had a chance to take part in the recent decline. However, maybe you don't realize that you've been affected. Maybe you have demand-type loans, the type that investors and businesspeople use. The interest rate on these loans changes every time the prime lending rate is adjusted. But, maybe you borrowed money using a loan where the interest rate was high because you had little collateral. Now you have lots to offer a lender.

Borrowers in these situations should take a close look at their loans as they may not have to pay these high interest rates. In fact, they may be able to negotiate a lower interest rate than they are presently paying.

Why? Well, interest rates are based on the general market scenario and the credibility of the borrower. If you borrowed when you were in a poor negotiating position you may be able to cut a better deal right now. Or, if you have a high rate loan coming due right now you may be in position to renew it at a better rate than you presently pay.

In addition, if you believe that interest rates are still high and will fall in coming years, you may want to negotiate your way out of fixed-term loans into variable-rate loans where your rates will fall with the bank rate and prime lending rate. Many people borrow money to buy cars, appliances, furniture, etc., using consumer loans. In fact, many consumers buy these goods on their credit card limits, where interest rates are far higher than anywhere else in the industry. The rate charged on a personal loan is often lower than that charged on a consumer loan and generally far lower than you pay on a credit card balance.

Recognizing this, what better time to renegotiate than right now?

Many people remember the stock market massacre of October 1987. However, since then stock and mutual fund values have risen substantially. And real estate prices appear to have not even been affected by the stock market selloff. If you lodged any form of collateral to borrow money in the last year or so you might be able to argue with your lender that it's worth substantially more right now than it was when you struck your deal. If so, you should be able to justify that you are a better risk and, as a result, that you should be able to borrow at a lower interest rate.

Maybe you agreed to pay prime plus 2% when you originally borrowed. Now your credit rating has improved substantially, so you can negotiate a better interest rate. It might be that your income has risen substantially. Or maybe the value of the collateral you lodged as security has appreciated in value or maybe you've paid down your loan by a substantial amount. If you are involved in any of these situations you might be in position to lower your interest rate by enough to offset past interest rate increases.

Yet, few Canadians will take the time to renegotiate with their lenders no matter how much the situations change.

You see, lenders lend money on the best terms they can arrange. Once the loan is in place, at the terms arranged, there is no obligation on their part to voluntarily change the rate on your loans. However, it's a different story if you request a review. But it's up to you.

What if only one spouse worked when the loans were arranged but now there are two working spouses? The family income has risen, so you are a better risk. Rather than simply using part or all of the second income to pay down your loans, why not also go to your banker and try for a lower interest rate? The family income is higher and the loans will be paid down faster so you pose less risk. Maybe you now fit the lender's formula better and can arrange for one lower rate first mortgage to replace the existing first and second mortgages.

High interest rates are not a problem for those whose loans are not coming due for renewal. But, maybe you could actually lower your loan rates by negotiating with your lender. And, if you do have a loan that is coming due for renewal or you are about to take out one at today's rates, maybe you can negotiate a better deal simply by presenting a better case.

51

Save on Taxes When Selling Your House

Canadians are big movers. In fact, we move on average every three years. Some never move so that distorts the average a bit. However, most of us do move several times in our lifetimes.

When you do it might be an opportunity to save some taxes. You see, property law says that a family's principal residence is jointly owned by both spouses. That means that the proceeds from a house sale can be split evenly between both spouses. It also means that each spouse will be able to invest his or her half of the proceeds to earn investment income that's taxed at a lower rate, if, in fact, it's taxed at all.

The problem, though, is that many of the people who sell a house plan to move into another one. That means that they'll want the money to help pay for the new house. However, in some cases they may have other investments built up in the higher-income spouse's name. If so, they should consider selling them to help pay for the new house and letting the lower-income spouse keep his or her share of the proceeds from the original sale. Effectively, they've been able to transfer money for investment from a higher-income spouse to one who will be able to invest it with a lower tax liability.

For some families this type of transaction happens regularly. Their house rises in value at the same time as they pay off their mortgage. They sell the house and move into a similarly priced one. The proceeds are split.

It's especially useful for those who are downsizing or retiring. Splitting the income means less tax on the income.

To show you how well this can work take a look at these numbers. If both spouses worked there's no question that you can justify an equal split of all the proceeds from a house sale. Let's assume that you sell a $200,000 house. Rather than leaving all the money in one spouse's name, you should split it — $100,000 to the husband and the other $100,000 to the wife.

But, what if you want to buy another house? In this example the husband, who is the higher-income earner, should use his $100,000 to buy a house. As a result, the wife can invest her monies without any fear of the income being taxed in her husband's name.

Maybe you aren't ready to downsize. As a result, a $100,000 house wouldn't satisfy you. In that case it would pay for the husband to take on a mortgage, or better yet, sell some investments so that he could buy the house mortgage free.

Ah ha, but maybe you like the investments you own. Well, don't worry. You don't have to get rid of them. Simply sell them to your spouse. Now you as a family still own them. Besides, your spouse was going to have to invest the money somewhere, right? It might as well be in something you like.

And, if you want to buy some investments you have $200,000 (in this example) of paid-up equity in your house. If you borrow against it you have a tax-deductible investment loan.

If only one of you worked, it can be argued that only the worker contributed to the house. In that case a divorce would still give your spouse one half of the equity. So, why shouldn't it work if you aren't getting a divorce? In the worst case scenario you should have no trouble justifying transferring one half of all the appreciation over and above the original purchase price to your spouse.

52

When You Sell Your House, Try Not to Take a Vendor-Take-Back Loan

When it's tough to find a buyer for your house, especially when interest rates are high, it's not uncommon for homeowners to offer low-rate financing to attract a buyer. This practice is called vendor-assisted financing or a vendor-take-back mortgage. As a vendor, avoid it whenever possible, as you can end up in a major tax jackpot.

Here's what happens. When you lend somebody money you earn interest. Interest used to be tax free until we exceeded $1,000, but that's no longer possible as a result of tax reform. The income received on a vendor-take-back loan in taxable and must be claimed. As a result, you've offered a lower-than-normal rate of interest in the first place and get to keep even less of it after you've paid your tax bill.

You'd be better off taking the money and investing it in stocks, mutual funds or rental real estate where you can earn a higher rate or return. And what if you're planning to buy another house? If you don't get all cash for your house, you'll have to take on a larger-than-normal mortgage when you buy your new one. The interest you earn on your VTB will be taxable but the interest you pay on your new mortgage will not be tax deductible as it isn't a business or investment loan.

You'll end up paying twice as much on your new loan as you earn on the one granted to the purchaser of your property. So, try to avoid vendor-assisted financing when you're the vendor.

53

If You Are Giving a Vendor-Take-Back Loan, Use the Bank's Money or Your Self-Directed RRSP

It's wonderful that the decline in interest rates over the last year has made it much easier for those who want to sell their houses — and more affordable for those who wish to buy. But, many homeowners are still finding they have to offer low-interest-assisted financing to find a buyer. Vendor-take-back mortgages at a lower than market rate are a valuable selling tool but they definitely can produce some tax problems if they aren't handled properly.

Consider this situation. An individual arranges to sell his house but is obliged to give a $50,000 vendor-take-back mortgage to close the deal. Yes, he has sold his house. But, now he has to dump the vendor-take-back mortgage on the open market at less than $50,000 as it earns less than other investments. He may not even be able to claim a capital loss unless he has already exceeded his $100,000 tax-free capital gains deduction.

If he chooses to hang onto the VTB he now owns a subpar investment as far as yield is concerned. And, if he doesn't have enough cash to buy his new house because he didn't receive cash for the one he just sold, he will now have to take on a larger mortgage. The interest on that mortgage will not be tax deductible because it was taken to buy a principal residence. This is like double jeopardy. You earn less than you pay out and the interest you earn is taxable even though the interest you pay out is not tax deductible.

Most people will endure this predicament even though they don't necessarily have to. It may be that they think it's only for a short period of time or that it can't be avoided. But, many could ease or eliminate this tax bite.

If you're caught in this predicament try this strategy. Approach your banker and ask to borrow the amount of the VTB upfront. It might be a personal loan, it might involve increasing the size of your first mortgage or may even be a second mortgage. Either way you now have enough money to lend to the purchaser of your house. He or she will now be able to give it to you as part of the purchase price of your house. You receive it tax free as it's simply part of the price of your principal residence. You now get all the cash you need to buy your new house so you have a smaller mortgage or none at all. That saves you non-tax-deductible interest.

You do have to pay interest, though. You borrowed money to lend to your buyer. He or she is paying you interest so you should be able to justify this as a tax-deductible investment loan. The interest you pay will be a tax deduction against the interest you earn and will go a long way toward eliminating the tax bill. Unless interest rates fall further you will probably pay a higher interest rate on your loan than you earn. However, this strategy, by eliminating the tax liability, will bring you very close to breaking even. You should, though, do your very best to make any vendor-take-back loans short term. You've sold your house. You don't want to worry about whether or not you are going to get your money. In fact, if the purchaser doesn't pay you may end up with no choice but to take the house back in a bad market. Now you have two houses.

Another strategy involves your registered retirement savings plan. If you have money in an RRSP it can be used to mortgage real estate in Canada. We don't generally recommend you use your RRSP for personal mortgages because of the fees. In this case, though, it might make a little more sense.

You need a self-directed RRSP at an institution that allows mortgages as one of the accepted investments. Now all you have to do is arrange for your RRSP to lend enough money to your purchaser so he or she can pay for your house. This purchaser will also have to pay interest on this loan but it will be earned tax free inside your RRSP. At the end of the loan's term your purchaser will pay any remaining principal into your registered retirement savings plan tax free as it's simply the return of the plan's money. You once again, though, have a tax advantage in that you (through your RRSP) earn tax-free interest at the same time as you pay out less non-tax-deductible interest.

The problem with these strategies is that they involve fees. For a very short term strategy the fees may not be worth it. However, the more money involved the more justifiable the fees.

With the personal loan strategy you will want a lawyer to arrange the mortgage. Those fees may be paid by the borrower or they may be small if rolled in with the rest of your closing costs. With the self-directed RRSP loan you have a $100-a-year RRSP fee. Many of us already pay this fee so it may not be an extra cost. However, you will have to pay the institution a fee of about $250 a year to administer the mortgage. That's another reason why you will want this to be over within a short period of time.

Even with the fees, though, the tax savings can make it well worth your while.

54

Drop a Vendor-Take-Back Mortgage When the Rates Fall

It's not uncommon for a vendor to offer a take-back mortgage to the purchaser of his house, especially when interest rates are high. It makes it easier for the vendor to sell his house because the terms of a VTB mortgage are usually more attractive than a lender's would be. The problem, though, is that the vendor normally faces a tax problem when this is done. The interest received on the mortgage loan is taxable now that the $1,000 tax-free investment income deduction has been cancelled. At the same time, if the vendor has been forced to take on a second mortgage or a larger loan when purchasing another house, the interest paid on that loan won't be tax deductible as it was taken to buy a principal residence and not an investment or business.

When interest rates fall, though, two things can happen. Number one, the borrower may be happy to get out of the VTB. Maybe he or she can now combine the VTB and the normal first mortgage into one mortgage at today's new lower interest rates. Or maybe the borrower has the cash to outright pay it off.

The second possibility is that the vendor might be able to sell the VTB mortgage on the open market. If interest rates fall far enough, the loan may now be higher than the going interest rates at commercial lenders. When that happens, investors may be prepared to buy it from the vendor at the full face value. Normally when the interest rate of a mortgage doesn't match existing interest rates, an investor will offer a discounted price, i.e., something lower than face value. However, when interest rates are low, the vendor has a better chance of getting all his money back. Then that money can be used to pay down a mortgage. Taxes are saved plus the mortgage payments become tax deductible.

55

Buy a House for a Student

So, your daughter has returned to university and you are appalled at the high cost of off-campus rent she has to pay. Landlords in college towns can do very well. Have you considered becoming one yourself? That's right. If you are going to have to house her anyway, and if real estate historically goes up in value over the years why not buy a house where your daughter can live with her friends? You will charge them rent similar to what they would pay elsewhere, and your daughter will manage the property for you.

The rationale is good especially in today's depressed real estate markets. More parents, in fact, are looking at it as a way to not only defray the cost of a university education but also to profit at the same time.

Take a few minutes to tally up the cost of a university education. There's tuition, books, transportation and living expenses. The latter will produce a healthy bite. If you break out the rent and multiply it by four or five you'll have a pretty good idea of how much money you'll have at your disposal to pay for mortgage, utilities and other expenses. Now all you have to do is come up with the down payment.

Part of the strategy here is to provide a comfortable residence for your child, part is to ease the expense and another major part is to get some tax relief. You see, if handled properly, we can even save taxes.

Regardless of the fact that you intend to rent part of this property to a daughter, this will still be treated as a normal rental real estate transaction. You will be able to claim all the interest you pay on mortgages and loans as a tax deduction plus all your maintenance, insurance, utilities, upkeep, etc., and maybe even capital cost allowance (depreciation) if you are making a profit. One of the expenses you would often incur when you have a rental property where there are a number of tenants would be a salary for a property manager. There's no reason why that can't be paid to your daughter. After all, she is protecting, managing and maintaining your investment. Therein lies the interesting tax twist.

Most rental real estate investments will give you the general tax deductions. This slant allows you to pay your child a salary. It will be tax deductible to you and probably not taxable to her as she will normally have only a small income from summer or part-time employment. If she has enough income to be taxable she will still be able to claim her tuition and the full-time student tax credit. That may be enough to make her non-taxable and even get her back onside as a dependant exemption.

Many taxpayers claim rental expenses incorrectly. They use them to offset rental income. Once their rental income reaches zero they forget the rest. You are allowed, though, to claim this negative rental income as a deduction against your salary. As a result, you can lower your taxable income by claiming negative rental income even though you paid your daughter a salary.

With any investment it's also important to look at the existing marketplace. Right now real estate prices are flat. They enjoyed a spring rally but the summer months have levelled off. This is a good time to buy. Neighborhoods near universities and colleges are good places to buy rental properties as there's normally a demand for rental space. In addition, there will undoubtedly be more parents who will catch onto this idea in future years so there should be a growing list of buyers looking to pay a fair dollar for your property four years or so down the road. You may not want to sell that soon if the market isn't right or if you have another student following in your daughter's footsteps. You may prefer to continue renting to other students. The longer you own the property the better your chance for profits.

Normally, we can expect the profits to be tax free. All Canadians are allowed to earn up to $100,000 in a lifetime of tax-free capital gains. If you haven't yet reached that level the gains earned here would qualify even though you paid your daughter a salary. If you have used your limit the gains will still be taxed at a lower rate than would be salary or interest income if you left your money in the bank.

There's one other possibility. If you put the house in your daughter's name she might be able to claim it as her principal residence. It would rise in value completely tax free. When she graduated she would be able to sell it and give the proceeds back to you or have a great start on a new residence where she chose to work. In this example a condo might be a better bet as it requires little maintenance. A house that is primarily rented out might create a problem when claimed as a principal residence.

It's an education in schooling and real estate.

56

A Retirement Home Can Be Tax Deductible

Many Canadians like to spend the winters in a warm climate when they retire. The problem, though, is that they don't plan ahead. They wait until they actually retire to buy or start to rent. Then they pay the going price — and they do it all themselves. Had they done a little planning in advance they may have been able to lock in to prices that were in vogue many years earlier, they may have been able to generate some tax deductions and they may have been able to get somebody to pay for their retirement home.

Rather than thinking of purchasing a house in Florida just before you retire, think of buying it as a rental property. When you buy a rental property the interest and other expenses are normally tax deductible. The same applies to a rental home in Florida or Hawaii or wherever you plan to retire. In addition, you'll be able to rent the property out until the time you choose to retire. That rental income, while taxable, will end up tax free when the expenses incurred while owning the property are used to offset it.

If the losses exceed the income, the remainder can be used as a deduction against your other income. In that case the taxman pays for part of the cost of your retirement home. When the income exceeds the expenses, the renters are paying for the property. Either way you've locked in today's prices rather than waiting and either the taxman or the tenants have picked up much of the cost.

When it's time to move in you do so, but at a fraction of the cost you'd pay had you waited.

57

We Can Make Our Mortgages Tax Deductible If We Want

Most Canadians pay their mortgage payments with tax-paid dollars. That is, they work all day to earn enough to pay their monthly mortgage payments. However, they forget that the taxman takes a portion of their salary before they get it. That means that we pay our mortgages with "after-tax" dollars. There is a way, though, to make our mortgages tax deductible — and as a result, get the taxman to pick up part of the cost.

If you have a mortgage and also have investment income, you may be in double jeopardy. That is, your investment income is taxable at the same time as your mortgage interest isn't tax deductible. If so, you should consider selling your investments to pay off your mortgage.

Once you do so, though, you may all of a sudden wish you had some money to invest. But, you do. You have a house with a small, or no, mortgage, so why not take advantage of the built-up equity to arrange a new loan to buy investments? When you do that the loan will be classed as an investment loan and the interest will be tax deductible. Don't think that you have to wait until you've paid off your mortgage, though. In fact, the individual with a $50,000 mortgage who also has $5,000 in savings or investments has the makings of a tax-deductible mortgage.

This individual should consider cashing in the $5,000 worth of investments and using the proceeds to pay down the mortgage. Then he or she can take a $5,000 personal loan, a second mortgage or increase the first mortgage back up to $50,000. If the $5,000 is then invested, that portion of your loan is now tax deductible. In this example, $5,000 of your $50,000 mortgage or 10% of it is tax deductible.

All you have to do then is calculate the interest portion of your mortgage payments and claim 10% as a tax deduction when you complete your tax return.

In coming years you can repeat the process to make even more of your mortgage tax deductible.

58

Another Way to Make Your Mortgage Tax Deductible

Who says we have to pay the high cost of mortgages and who says we can't afford to buy a house because prices are rising too quickly? Well, it certainly isn't me, because I believe we can get the taxman to help us do both — and we can get somebody else to pay much of the cost of the house.

Sound impossible? It isn't. It might not work for everybody, but for many, using these theories would wipe out much of the pain of mortgage rates and the inability to afford a house.

Under existing legislation most personal mortgages are not tax deductible. As a result, we pay a much higher real interest rate than we realize. In fact, the average taxpayer (in the 35% tax bracket) has to pay a real rate of 17% when he or she has an 11% mortgage. Because the payments are not tax deductible, we have to earn the equivalent of 17% when we have an 11% mortgage. Because the payments are not tax deductible, we have to earn the equivalent of 17% to be left with 11% after our employer remits tax to Ottawa and the provincial governments.

But if we could make our mortgages tax deductible we could make it a lot easier to own a home. And if we could get somebody else to pick up part of the cost of ownership we could make it a lot easier, and Revenue Canada is quite prepared to help us with both ideas.

To make the interest we pay on our mortgages tax deductible, all we have to do is convince Revenue Canada that we borrowed the money to make money. They're quite prepared to be our partners if they think they'll share in a windfall down the road.

Recognizing that, we might be wise to buy a duplex or triplex that we rent out, even if we choose to live in part of it. For example, if we purchased a triplex and lived in one unit we would be justified in claiming two thirds of our interest expense as a tax deduction. The other third would be a personal expense, but our real mortgage cost has now fallen substantially.

But, there's more. The rents earned on the other two units will offset most of the other expenses related to owning this real estate. That is, the renters will help to carry the cost of owning your property at the same time as the taxman helps with the mortgage. In addition, when we own rental property, we are allowed to claim the heat, hydro, property taxes and other legitimate expenses as tax deductions. If we want to advertise for tenants, incur legal bills to get rid of them or to collect the rents, we again will get some tax relief.

You see, if you feel you can't afford to buy a house right now, why not consider buying a multiple unit property so you get some tax relief and somebody else to help with the bills?

So far it doesn't sound too bad. But, before you start calling real estate agents don't forget that you will be giving up some privacy, you will have to do or arrange to have somebody take care of the maintenance and you will have to accept the fact that while a principal residence will rise in value completely free of tax, a rental unit does not.

Ah, but even when we sell this property we get a break. You see, even though the federal government has gone back on its word and reduced our tax-free capital gains limit from $500,000 to only $100,000, we still come out a winner. If we decide sometime in the future to remove the tenants and convert the property to a single family residence we may not have to pay any tax after all, even though Revenue Canada considers this the equivalent to outright selling the property. In the first place, one-third of the gain will be tax free as the property was used as our principal residence. The remainder of the gain will qualify for the $100,000 tax-free capital gains deduction, and if the property were jointly owned by both spouses, the first $200,000 in gains will be tax free. That should eliminate most, if not all, of your tax bills.

If, instead of renovating, you choose to sell the property, the same theory applies. However, a rental property in a good area will generally attract a larger audience and price than will a single family home. Now you'll be able to take the proceeds and buy your dream house. The advantages have been substantial. To begin with, you've been able to buy at today's prices. As a result, any future increases are in your favor rather than against you. You've enjoyed some tax relief, somebody else has picked up part of the cost of ownership, and any increase in price has been tax free. What more could you ask for?

59

Don't Mortgage Your Property Taxes

Many homeowners have no choice. When they buy a house, the lending institution demands that they include in their mortgage payment enough money to service not just their interest and principal but also their property taxes.

While that's not a bad idea if you think you'll have problems paying your tax bill on time, it is a bad idea financially speaking. You see, when you make all your monthly payments on time you will generally have more money in your tax account than you need. It might be nice to have that cache sitting there to protect you when tax rates rise, but it's also just as easy to increase your mortgage payment.

In many cases, you see, your mortgage anniversary or renewal date will coincide with a tax adjustment. As a result, you normally don't need to build up a balance in your tax account. All you have to do is budget for a slight increase.

The real drawback, of course, is that while the money is sitting on deposit at the financial institution, it's earning a very low rate of return, if, in fact, the lender pays you any interest at all. Instead, the extra balance could be paid against your outstanding principal, which would pay it off faster than normal. And, what's worse, when you fall behind in your tax account the lender adds the shortfall to your loan. That can mean that you end up paying interest on that amount for the rest of the life of the mortgage.

It's a two-sided street when you add your property taxes to your mortgage payment. If you feel you'll keep abreast of your tax requirements you should try to pay them separately. If you fear you'll fall behind, pay them together. If you choose that route try not to keep too much cash tied up in your tax account

— and whatever you do don't fall behind. If you fall behind, you may pay interest on the amount along with the rest of your loan for the rest of the life of the mortgage.

Once you've paid off your mortgage and decide to remortgage to buy investments, you seldom have this problem.

60

When You Move, Do It Right

How would you like to get paid to move? Many of us can, even though many don't bother to ask — and many others could but don't because they failed to set up their affairs properly.

The summer is always a big time of year for the moving industry. Many Canadians try to time their move for early summer so they cause the least possible pain for their children. Many others wait until the end of summer, especially this year. Once interest rates started to fall many people jumped into the real estate markets trying to snap up the bargains. In addition, thanks to the recession and the shortage of jobs more Canadians than usual are moving from depressed areas to those where there's a better chance for employment.

Many of these people can get some tax relief on their moving costs if they plan properly.

The best move is to get your boss to pay for it. Moving expenses are tax deductible for employers and not a taxable benefit for employees. As a result, it's best to get your employer to pay as many of the expenses as possible. Where you can, try to arrange for your employer to pay for the lion's share of the expenses, leaving you with the proper items that can then be claimed as tax-deductible moving expenses in your own name.

Small businesspeople and self-employed types who have operated a business out of their premises should be able to claim some of their moving expenses as a business expense. If you run a landscaping business out of your garage and you move to a house with a bigger garage you should be able to prorate your moving expenses to take this into consideration.

Employees who move can also qualify to write off the bulk of their expenses if they meet the right criteria. Two things are required and they *both* must be met. You must move so that your new place of residence is at least 40 kilometres closer to your new job than was your old residence. Did you notice the catches? Not only must you move but you must also take on a new job. Lots of us move but not everybody moves to take on a new job. In addition, you don't have to move 40 kilometres, you have to move so that your new house is at least 40 kilometres closer to your new job than is your old one. Moving from one city to another seldom creates a problem. However, moving across town may not meet the 40-kilometre requirement. This year, though, more people are able to meet both criteria as they move across the country looking for work.

What qualifies as a moving expense? The list is long. It's important that you contact the local Revenue Canada office and get their information on moving expenses. When you file your tax return you will have to include form T-1M so you might as well familiarize yourself with it right now.

When you look at this information you'll see that the normal expenses like packing and transporting your goods are included. On occasion, movers won't touch perishable items like frozen foods and plants. You will have to carry them yourself or dispose of them since Revenue Canada allows you no loss if they are damaged.

If you sold a house to move to a new one you can claim some extra expenses. Included are legal bills and real estate commissions and any penalties incurred to break a mortgage. Moving expenses can be pretty hefty. When you add on the last three items you can be in for some sizable tax savings so make sure you do it properly.

The cost of transporting you and your household to your new location are also deductible. "Household" is an important word here as it goes further than "family." It includes other people who live with you, like a nanny. And, it includes animals. If you have to buy a cage, sedate the animal, pay extra transportation costs, these are all tax deductible. You will also be able to claim transportation expenses like gas, oil, meals, lodging and taxes for up to 15 days so make sure you keep every receipt you can.

You don't have to include them with your tax return but you may be called upon to produce them at a later date.

If you transport your vehicles rather than drive (this includes cars, trucks, boats and mobile homes) the transportation cost is included and you will still be able to claim the cost of airfare, bus, train, etc., including the cost of getting to and from the airport. When you arrive at your new home you also get some tax relief. If you sold a home to move and now buy a home you will be able to claim your land transfer taxes and legal fees. If you didn't sell a house you won't enjoy these deductions. However, you can claim the cost of breaking a lease.

The last catch is that these expenses can only be claimed against work-type income earned at your new place of employment. If you move late in the year you may not be able to claim them all this year. Not to worry, they can be carried forward to next year.

61

Students Can Claim Tax-Deductible Moving Expenses

When the students go back to school don't forget that they can qualify for moving expense deductions just as we can when we move to take a new job. The rationale behind claiming moving expenses as a tax deduction is that we made the move to earn taxable income. Revenue Canada benefits in the long run so they help us out to get there.

It stands to reason then that students who move home, or anywhere for that matter, to take a summer job should be able to claim their moving costs as a tax deduction. But what about moving expenses when you go back to school? Well, the answer is that they also qualify — in some cases. If you earn a scholarship, bursary, fellowship or work grant this type of income is considered "work related." You are going to school to get this income. As a result, your moving expenses to get back to school will be tax deductible.

Be careful, though. The first $500 of this type of income is tax free. There's no place to declare this deduction on your tax return. You simply deduct it from the total income and declare the remainder on your return. Then you get to claim your moving expenses.

If you move to attend postsecondary school in a foreign country your expenses will still qualify. And, if you move to Canada from another country make sure you keep all your receipts because, likewise, you will be able to claim moving expenses as a tax deduction.

Many people move to more prosperous regions to seek out work. Moving expenses are acceptable as tax deductions even though you don't actually have a job to which you are going.

However, they are only deductible against the income you earn in that new job. Unfortunately, they are not deductible against unemployment insurance even though we paid premiums to provide UIC. The same predicament applies to investment income. Many people move across the country looking for work, and until they find it, they live off investment income, often exhausting their savings. Again, they will get no tax relief against that type of income.

When it comes to using moving expense deductions it's important to look at the financial planning aspect. It may not appear important for a student to look at these expenses, but, it can be extremely rewarding for a parent or a spouse. The net income line on our tax returns is gradually becoming the most important line. It determines whether or not we get to claim our children or spouse as dependant exemptions. Moving expenses are claimed before the net income line. If we can lower our child's or spouse's net income to the point where we get them back onside as a tax deduction we become a winner.

The taxable income line also plays a role in our thinking. If a student can lower his or her taxable income to zero the person who supports the student will be able to claim leftover tuition and the $10 per month full-time student tax credit. It's important to claim any moving expenses first, then any tuition or other deductions to lower both the net income and taxable income lines. It's especially important when the student is a spouse because the spousal deduction is far higher than the tax relief offered by a dependent child. And, don't forget the equivalent to married exemption. If you are a single parent supporting a child 18 or under you may be able to claim the student at the spousal rate. Now the tax advantages of properly claiming moving expenses and tuition take on much more importance.

If you move to take on employment it's also important that you consider financial planning between you and your spouse. You see, moving expenses can only be claimed against income earned at your new job. The later you move the less room you'll have this year. The remainder will have to carried over to next year, which means you'll get the tax relief a year later. However, moving expenses can be split between spouses in any ratio that seems reasonable provided both spouses qualify. If both of you get work you can both claim some of the expenses this year, if, of course, it's to your value.

Let's say one spouse is in a very low tax bracket. It might be valuable to claim some of the moving expenses in that person's name. If his or her net income were lowered enough you may get to claim the spousal exemption. However, if one spouse is in a very high tax bracket it might be better to claim some expenses this year in that spouse's name and carry the remainder over to next year. Even though you get your tax relief a year later it may be far greater in dollar value than claiming any in the lower income spouse's name.

Because moving expenses can be very large you may even want to consider removing an equivalent amount of money from your RRSP. Your taxable income will be knocked down by the moving expenses and only come back to normal when your RRSP withdrawal is added on. Effectively, you will have been able to remove a chunk of money from your RRSP tax free.

62

Save Taxes by Picking the Right Month to Move

Many of us can't pick and choose a time to move because our employer tells us when to do it. Those who can, though, may be able to save some tax dollars by picking the right time of year.

The Canadian tax system has us pay our federal taxes first. Then we pay an additional portion of those taxes to the government in the province where we live on the final day of the year. What's even more important, though, is the realization that the percentage we pay this provincial government varies from province to province. It doesn't matter whether we live in the highest-taxed province most of the year; we'll pay the tax rate in the province where we reside on the last calendar day of the year.

Knowing this, we can wisely choose our proper course when we're planning a move late in the year.

Tax rates change from year to year. However, we can normally count on only small changes to the positioning of provinces in their order of taxability. We used to recommend that individuals move from the east, where taxes are higher, to the west, where they are lower, as the year end approached. With both federal and provincial tax reform changing the federal rates and provincial rates, this rule of thumb doesn't quite work any longer. However, it's relatively easy to track the provincial rates — which can help us decide to move from any province to another.

Following are the combined federal and provincial tax rates for each province and territory. Because we pay tax at the rate applied by the province where we live on December 31 of any year, it pays to move from a high-rated province before the year ends. Conversely, it pays to delay any move from a low-taxed province to one where rates are higher until the beginning of a new year.

When looking at these numbers, consider that you are a taxpayer with $30,000 in taxable income. That is, you've used every tax deduction you can and still have $30,000 on which to pay tax. The next dollar you earn will be taxed at the rates shown. However, don't get caught in the trap of thinking that these numbers are the maximum you can earn. The highest tax rates generally click in at around $55,000 in taxable income — with Ontario and P.E.I. initiating their highest rates above $85,000.

Quebec	50.5%
Manitoba	50.4
Nova Scotia	50.3
Saskatchewan	49.8
P.E.I.	49.5
Newfoundland	49.3
New Brunswick	48.7
Ontario	48.2
Alberta	46.4
B.C.	46.3
Yukon	44.4
N.W.T.	44.1

Using this theory, it would pay for a taxpayer who had some flexibility in timing to move from Quebec to the Yukon before the end of a year. Even though his or her employer has been withholding taxes at the higher rates levied in Quebec, the taxpayer would only have to pay tax on the full year's income at the lower rates levied in the Yukon (or any other province chosen). As a result, the taxpayer would be in for a sizable tax rebate.

And, just in case you don't think it means very much, a move of this nature would save the taxpayer more than $2,500.

Conversely, moving in the wrong direction (that is, from a low-taxed province to one where rates are high) would cost you additional taxes on all the income earned that year.

Granted, not everybody moves late in the year and not everybody can dictate their moving date. But, where possible, you can save yourself a sizable chunk of tax dollars by doing a little research before you make your move. A good chat with your employer about the timing of your move may be all that's necessary. After all, your boss wants a happy employee. A little extra cash can be very helpful.

63

When You Move, It Doesn't Always Pay to Sell

Canadians regularly get transferred from one job to another. When we move, we normally sell our existing house and buy a new one in the city where we're relocating.

Sometimes, though, it can pay to hang onto the old house as well as buying the new house. Naturally, finances will play a role — but so does the taxman.

If you do have the resources to handle two properties and if you think there's any chance that you'll get transferred back to the city where you own house number one, you can profit from a special four-year provision. It allows you to claim two properties as your principal residence over that time period.

Actually, now that we have a capital gains tax holiday most people can own two or more houses without worrying about tax. One is legitimately classed as a tax-free principal residence. The other or others won't trigger capital gains until you sell them, and then most of the gains will be tax free under the capital gains tax holiday.

However, if you can use the special four-year principal residence rule, you'll come out even further ahead.

In either case here's what happens. If you move to a new residence it will be treated as your principal residence. As a result, it will rise in value totally tax free. In addition, any gains won't erode the $100,000 of capital gains that you're entitled to earn in a lifetime. Nor will they affect the minimum tax rules.

At the same time, if you were able to hang onto house number one, you could get some tax relief. If you rented it out to somebody else they'd cover most or all of the operating expenses. As a result, you wouldn't have to worry too much about carrying costs. In addition, all the expenses you paid would be tax deductible — first, against the rental income, and secondly, against other forms of income. As a result, any expenses not paid by the renters could end up as tax deductions on your tax return.

But real estate generally rises in value. That, of course, is one of the reasons why you'd use this idea — because you felt that house number one was going to jump in value in coming years. You knew you maintained it well and that it wouldn't create any problems. And you'd even like to live in it again sometime.

If this property does rise in value, you'll earn a tax-free capital gain on top of having the tenants pay most of the costs. That's not a bad deal.

By the way, when it comes to making this move it's best to leave maximum mortgage financing in place on house number one. As it's going to be a rental property, the interest on that mortgage will be tax deductible.

You also want to raise as much cash as possible for house number two. It's going to be your principal residence so the mortgage interest won't be tax deductible.

You also want to raise as much cash as possible for house number two. It's going to be your principal residence so the mortgage interest won't be tax deductible. As a result, you want as small a mortgage as possible.

If you use the four-year rule you get a bonus. The gain in value in both houses can be claimed as part of your principal residence. As a result, neither will affect your $100,000 tax-free capital gains. So don't always sell when you move.

64

Strategies for Your Fifties

The older we get the more cautious we should become when it comes to managing our money. We don't want to lose the assets we've accumulated to date but, by the same token, we don't want to let them stagnate to the point where they won't produce any future benefit. That's why it's probably more important for those in their 50s to get a handle on their financial requirements than anybody else. The young have plenty of time to make mistakes, although they will make substantial gains the sooner they start. Older individuals are terrible restricted in their options, so the sooner they start the better chance they have.

It's imperative that those in their 50s use as many tax deductions and tax deferrals as they can. That will give them more to work with. It's also important that they rid themselves of unnecessary expenses as quickly as possible so they have money to invest to produce future assets to generate retirement income. After all, they are 10 to 15 years away from retirement when their income levels will normally decline.

The very first consideration would be to do a budget check. Track your money for a month or two to see where it's going. Unless you know what you're doing with it you won't know whether you're making mistakes. The next step is to look hard and long at your tax situation. You can expect yearly salary increases between now and retirement, but will they be greater than the rate of inflation? Regardless, the more tax you can save in the next few years the more money you'll have to invest. When seeking out tax relief, though, you don't want to expose yourself to any more risk than is absolutely necessary.

That's why your company pension or registered retirement savings plan is so important at this stage. I say either as you may want to choose one over the other or you may want to combine the use of these plans.

It's not unusual for a company pension plan to provide a lower yield than is available through a personal RRSP. However, if your employer matches your contribution you can already be 50% ahead of an RRSP. As a result, it's important to compare the yields in the proper context before making your decision.

There's something else you should consider, especially at this age group. It's important to start moving money out of the higher-income spouse's name into the lower-income spouse's so that both spouses will have income as you approach retirement. Rather than having all the money taxed in one spouse's name each spouse will qualify for tax deductions, and when income becomes taxable it will be taxed at a lower rate if it's split between two tax returns rather than all lumped onto one. The RRSP will play an important role in this discussion as we have a choice whether we contribute to our own RRSP or one in our spouse's name.

It's called a spousal RRSP. The higher-income spouse will receive the tax deductions when he or she contributed to it, but the lower-income spouse will eventually draw a pension from it that will be taxed at that spouse's lower rate. And don't forget the pension-income deduction. Each Canadian taxpayer who receives pension income other than that sponsored by a government can claim the equivalent to the first $1,000 as tax-free income. You know your spouse will eventually receive the Old Age Security Pension and as a result will be lost to you as a dependant deduction. As a result you might as well plan for that day and arrange to get personal pension monies into his or her name through the use of a spousal RRSP. The first $1,000 will be tax free and the rest will be taxed at a lower rate than if it were earned in your own name.

If the lower-income spouse also has income or assets it's wise to consider letting that spouse keep all of his or her income and investments so they will produce income in coming years that will be taxed at a lower rate.

It's right about now that it becomes even more important to pay off your outstanding debts as quickly as possible. It's not as big a problem when you have tax deductible loans for investment purposes that are producing tax deductions and a decent yield at the same time. However, when the loan isn't tax deductible it costs you as much as twice the quoted interest rate. As a result, paying down your mortgage faster than normal right about now is a must. Don't forget also that under tax reform we can no longer earn $1,000 in tax-free investment income each year. So there's not much use accumulating an emergency savings plan when you have an outstanding mortgage. The interest you earn (generally at a lower rate than your mortgage costs) will be taxable while the interest you pay on your mortgage will not be tax deductible. It's called double jeopardy. If you ever run into a situation where you need money you'll have bargaining power with your banker as your mortgage will be smaller.

This is also the perfect time to look ahead to retirement, not from a financial standpoint, but from a location consideration. It's not uncommon for people to sell their homes and move into a rental unit at that time. Personally, I don't care for it, especially under tax reform which makes all interest income taxable. I'd rather see people in this position sell their houses and move into a condo. They don't have the maintenance and they still own a principal residence that's going to rise in value tax free, in addition to the tax-free capital gains we're entitled to earn. A nice trick, though, would be to buy the condo now and rent it out until you're ready to use it. The carrying costs would be tax deductible, creating tax relief against your salary, the tenants would cover the cost of owning the property, and more importantly, when it came time to move into it you'd find that you were way ahead as you'd purchased it at this year's price — not the inflation-effected prices in vogue 15 years or so down the road.

If you're planning this attack you might want to purchase your retirement home in the warm southern climes or at the lake, where you'll really be able to put your feet up and enjoy the benefits of the financial planning you did when you were in your 50s, the most important time of your life.

65

No Money? You Can Borrow for an RRSP

So, you like the idea of contributing to a registered retirement savings plan but you don't have the money. Should you bother to borrow or simply skip 1991's contribution.

Maybe you don't have to make this decision after all. You see, if you have a self-directed RRSP and you own some Canada Savings Bonds, term deposits, GICs, stocks or mutual funds you can contribute them instead of cash. Many taxpayers don't contribute to their RRSPs because they don't have the cash but they could have saved the same amount of tax by simply transferring in an equivalent amount of existing investments. Be careful, though, as you don't want to overcontribute. That is, calculate the amount of money you can contribute then total the present value of your investment. Let's say you are entitled to contribute $3,000 and you have a $3,000 CSB. If you contributed the full bond you would actually be contributing $3,000 plus the interest that had accrued since the day you purchased it. You would be over the $3,000 level. If you contribute stocks or mutual funds that have appreciated in value you can use the entire amount but any appreciation must also be considered a capital gain as if you sold the funds or stocks to somebody else. If you create a capital loss you are not allowed to claim the loss.

Others will have to decide whether it's advantageous to borrow. Here's how I look at it. Let's say you have the right to contribute $5,000 for 1991. You have to borrow the full amount. If you contribute the $5,000 to your RRSP you should get a tax rebate of about $2,000. If you pay the $2,000 tax rebate against your loan balance you will owe $3,000. As this loan is not tax deductible you'd be wise to pay it down as fast as possible. Let's say you pay $300 interest before the loan is paid off.

Inside your RRSP you will earn income with the entire $5,000. At 12% it would earn $600 in the year. If you bought good-quality mutual funds or stocks you should earn, on average, $900 or more. As a result, you should be able to double or triple your loan cost plus get a $2,000 or so tax rebate. So yes, the overwhelming answer is to borrow for your 1991 RRSP contribution if you don't have the cash.

Usually this type of loan is not tax deductible. However, some taxpayers can make the interest they pay a tax-deductible expense. Consider the individual who owns some investments that don't qualify for use inside an RRSP. If you sold these investments you could put the cash inside your RRSP. If you then borrowed to buy a similar investment, or the same one after a 30-day wait, you would now have an investment loan, not one used to contribute to an RRSP. The loan would now be tax deductible.

The same theory applies to a businessperson who could be using cash to contribute to an RRSP and borrowing money for business purposes. It's simply a matter of using the money for the right purposes.

Many other taxpayers face this question. Do I contribute to my RRSP or pay down my mortgage? I've long been a believer in paying off all non-tax-deductible loans as fast as possible. The mortgage is an especially important target as paying extra against a loan like this saves extra cash since it is such a long-term loan. However, when it comes to deciding whether to pay down a mortgage or contribute to an RRSP things get a little more complicated. If you pay $5,000, let's say, against a 12% mortgage you will have about $600 a year in interest. And, because you have now eliminated $5,000 of principal you will save this $600 every year for the rest of the life of the mortgage. Some people think this strategy shaves years off the end of their loans. However, it's really the fact that your regular mortgage payment instantly becomes too large that pays the loan down so much faster. In fact, each time you make a payment you pay extra against your principal, which means your next payment will do even more damage.

If you contribute $5,000 to your RRSP and earn 12% you will earn $600 a year inside your plan. And, it will compound tax free as long as it remains inside your plan. Effectively, this money should grow at the same rate as you save money if you pay down your mortgage provided you earn the same rate as your mortgage costs you or better.

Once you contribute to an RRSP you will get a tax rebate. In this example it should be something like $2,000. If you pay the yearly tax rebate against your mortgage you get the best of both worlds, an RRSP contribution that saves taxes and compounds tax free and a payment against your mortgage. Effectively, the taxman is paying down your loan at the same time as you are profiting.

66

Your RRSP: What Should Be Inside? Outside?

From time to time I hear or read of consultants who say that you should never put stocks or mutual funds inside a registered retirement savings plan. Well, the word "never" doesn't exist in my financial planning dictionary. There are times when I would do something and other times when I wouldn't, but to categorize something as "never" is too restricting.

One of the "never" reasons is that you might not sleep well at night. It's a valid complaint and suggests that you not only refrain from putting equity-based investments inside your RRSP, but that you don't hold them anywhere at all.

Another reason can be that this is the pool of money that you are going to use to produce a pension in your retirement. Exposing it to undue risk could reduce your pension at retirement time. That's a valid complaint if you are planning to invest this money for only a short period of time. However, it's a proven fact that exposure to real estate, the stock markets or mutual funds over a long period of time will virtually always produce more funds than interest-bearing investments. Yes, timing it right can give you a better start. But, over the long run, say 10 years or more, those who invest their money will do better than those who save it in an interest-bearing investment.

There is another common comment about investing your RRSP funds in equities, and, quite frankly, it has some merit. When we buy Canadian stocks or mutual funds outside our RRSPs we qualify for the dividend tax credit. This credit allows us to earn approximately $22,000 in tax-free dividends in a year if that's the only type of income we earn. Yet, if we earn dividends inside our RRSP we are not allowed to claim the dividend tax credit. As a result, it appears that there is some merit to this argument. You are better off owning stocks and mutual funds outside your RRSP than inside. In addition, if we own stocks, mutual funds or real estate outside our RRSPs we qualify for tax-free capital gains until we exceed $100,000 ($500,000 for small business investments and farms). Inside an RRSP capital gains can compound totally free of tax, but once we remove the money we must pay tax on it at our normal income tax rate.

On the surface, then, it would appear that this last argument holds water.

Before we dismiss it let's consider one more fact. Yes, I agree that you lose the dividend tax credit and the tax-free capital gains. But, what if you have other forms of income that water down the benefits of the dividend tax credit? And what if you've already exceeded the $100,000 in tax-free capital gains? In that case you will definitely want to get as much money into your RRSP as you can since whatever yield you earn will compound tax free.

But even with all these thoughts maybe there is another reason why you would want to invest the funds inside your RRSP in mutual funds and/or stocks. It's the yield. That's right. It's okay to think about the dividend tax credit and the tax-free capital gains. But what about the numbers? What do they say?

Well, if you contributed the maximum allowable amount to your RRSP each year from 1971 until now you would have contributed a total of $91,000 to your plan. If you chose any investment that purely matched the rate of inflation you would have $178,191 inside your plan. Had you chosen a savings account inside your plan you would have a total of $196,484. So, you exceeded the rate of inflation. If you chose a five-year guaranteed investment certificate you would have $248,815. A short-term money market investment would do slightly better at $250,027. But that's the end of the normal interest-bearing RRSP choices.

There are hundreds of mutual funds out there. Some win and some lose. Had you chosen what is normally accepted as Canada's most recognized mutual fund, Industrial Growth Fund, you would have accumulated, in this example, a grand total of

$489,326. That's almost twice the yield earned on any of the normal choices. Yes, I admit that it would be better to own this investment outside your RRSP where you would benefit from the dividend tax credit and the tax-free capital gains deduction. However, to say you shouldn't hold it inside your plan would clearly be wrong, since you would be limiting yourself to interest-bearing investments that over the last 20 years have produced about half the yield available from the fund.

There is no question that you do not get the dividend tax credit and capital gains inside the RRSP. However, if long-term records show that your could get twice as much money why wouldn't you go for it?

If you could earn a pension worth 10% of your principal, the fund would, in this example, give you $48,932.60 a year compared to $24,881.50 with the five year GIC. Which would you rather have?

67

Why Settle for One RRSP When Two May Be Better?

There's no question that anybody with taxable income should consider using a registered retirement savings plan. But why stop at one? There are some valid reasons for having at least two of these plans.

Consider the young female who's either married or considering marriage. She should be putting the maximum she can afford into her own RRSP. When she marries, she should continue doing so but, if she's planning a family, her husband should also put as much as he can afford into a spousal RRSP. Now she has a personal plan and also a spousal one.

Let's say she decides to have a family. She leaves work so she has no income, or at least very little. As a result, she has no tax burden. That means that she can start removing the money from her personal RRSP without having to pay much, if any, tax on the proceeds.

In fact, she should be able to remove all the money from her plan over a three-year period without paying much tax.

Now she can start removing the money her husband has been contributing to her spousal RRSP.

Don't forget that any time we remove money from a spousal RRSP, the tax can be payable by the spouse who contributed the money in the first place. We can, however, insure that the tax is paid by the lower-income spouse if we remember one easy-to-follow rule. In this example, it says that the husband won't have to pay tax on the money removed from his wife's spousal RRSP provided no money was removed until three years after he made his last contribution.

Well, that's easy enough to handle here. During the three years when his wife is removing from her personal RRSP, he can direct his contributions to a personal plan in his own name. Once she's removed all the money from her personal plan, she'll be able to start removing funds from her spousal plan and be taxed at her low tax rate because her husband has, in fact, skipped three years of contributions to her plan.

By this time, she may decide to go back to work. If so, the family can start all over again. She'll contribute to a personal plan while he contributes to a spousal plan in his wife's name. That way she'll have double the contributions coming in to help offset the money that was already removed.

Once again, the family is back to earning two sets of deductions — and in fact they may look at repeating the removal process again sometime down the road.

One thing to remember, though, is the spousal tax credit. Once a spouse exceeds $525 in net income he or she is gradually reduced as a dependant tax credit. In essence, any income earned by your spouse in excess of $525 (net income) will be taxed at your top marginal rate as you will lose one dollar's worth of tax deductions every time he or she earns another dollar. As a result, you will often find that it's best to remove less than $525 or jump the number to around the $10,000 range. The rationale is that the first $525 was tax free and the amount earned by your spouse after you lose him or her as a dependant is also taxed at a low rate (or none at all). The combination works well.

68

Don't Be Afraid to Spread Your RRSPs Around

How many registered retirement savings plans do you have? One or many? For many taxpayers the answer is "one" since they simply go back to the very same institution each year. For others, the answer can be "one" because they don't have enough money in their RRSP to worry about exceeding the deposit insurance coverage. Yet others may answer "one" because they have a self-directed plan. All these RRSP users could be making a mistake.

There's no set answer to the question. Some taxpayers who have more than one shouldn't, some who have only one should diversify, others should vary their investment mix. As a result, they definitely will want to seek out a self-directed plan.

One of the common reasons for having more than one RRSP is for security purposes. Those who consistently seek out interest-bearing deposits in their RRSPs have to consider the safety of their money. That's why they choose GICs and term deposits in the first place — they get deposit insurance coverage. However, it's only good on the first $60,000 of accumulated interest and principal. Those who exceed that amount should consider one of several choices. Either have several RRSPs where they keep less than $60,000 in each, open a self-directed RRSP that has term deposits or GICs of several companies inside or switch some investments into government bonds, mortgage-backed securities, Canada Savings Bonds or treasury bills.

One complaint against the self-directed plan at this stage is its yearly fee (in most cases about $100). However, if you have several RRSPs that charge administration fees, or if there is a premature cancellation fee or a fee to move your plan, you may find the self-directed fee isn't onerous after all.

Many Canadians earn less than they could when they stick with only one RRSP. They simply go back to the same institution each year and accept whatever rate they're offered. Yet, had they shopped around I'm sure they could have earned a much better rate of return. That doesn't mean you should open a new RRSP at a different institution each year, though. In fact, if the new institution you choose this year offers a better rate than you are already earning, why not switch all the money you have at other institutions to the new one?

In the past we used to recommend more than one RRSP for facility purposes. If you ever wanted any money out of your plan you had to cash the entire plan or go through some convoluted planning to get around this rule. However, in the fine print of the tax reform measures you'll find that it's now possible to remove part of the money from an RRSP. As a result, you no longer need more than one plan to satisfy this need.

Taxpayers with only small amounts in their RRSPs may also want to consider a self-directed plan. If you have all your money in a deposit-taking institution it may not be important. However, if some of your money is in stocks or mutual funds you may find a self-directed plan will save you fees even though you only have a small amount in your plan. Mutual funds charge trustee fees. If you have diversified into several funds you may be paying more than $100 a year in trustee funds already. Switching to a self-directed plan would ease your paperwork and may also cut your expenses. In fact, the more money you have inside your RRSP, the more value there is to using a self-directed plan. The fees look smaller all the time compared to the advantages gained.

Depending on the amount of money and the flexibility desired, a good case can be made for people never having more than one RRSP.

However, there are definitely examples where having more than one RRSP can be helpful. If you contribute to a spousal RRSP and your spouse also has earned income, it can be a mistake for that spouse to have only one plan. When you contribute to a spousal RRSP you will be taxed on any money removed within three years of your last contribution even though your spouse may have also been making contributions. He or she might want to remove some of the money he or she contributed but it would still be taxed at your rate. In this case it definitely pays for your spouse to contribute to one RRSP and you to another. When he or she wants money, compare which plan would produce the lower tax burden and remove the funds from that plan.

Starting last year, we are no longer able to contribute pension income into our own RRSP. We will be restricted to a maximum of $6,000 per year into a spousal RRSP. At that time it will become almost imperative that we have two RRSPS — one for personal use and one to accommodate the spousal transfers. At that time we may well want two RRSPs. Right now, though, it isn't always necessary.

69

Pay Down Your Mortgage While Building Up Your RRSP

Now that both interest rates and taxes are at very high levels, I'm constantly being questioned about what to do with mortgages and registered retirement savings plans. People want to save taxes but they also want to pay down their mortgages as fast as possible. One question, then, has to do with whether you should contribute to your RRSP or pay down your mortgage. The other explores whether you should use the money inside your RRSP to mortgage your house, or any other real estate, for that matter. The answers to both questions are tough and vary with each situation. However, thanks to an innovation these questions will be much easier to answer for most taxpayers and homeowners.

I normally recommend that taxpayers contribute to their RRSPS before they pay down their mortgages. The average Canadian in the 40% tax bracket would effectively save 40 cents on the dollar when he or she contributed to an RRSP, but only save 12 cents or so on a mortgage. Granted, it shaves future years of payments off the mortgage, but the funds inside the RRSP would compound to about the same amount as any savings on the mortgage. It is a controversial comparison, though. Under a new RRSP option there may no longer be a need to make this calculation.

The idea of arranging for your RRSP to mortgage your house sounds great. However, the fees involved are so high that it generally isn't worthwhile unless you have between $30,000 and $50,000 inside your RRSP. You have to pay $100 a year for a self-administered RRSP, and you need an approved institution to manage the mortgage, which might cost $250 a year. Finally, you need default insurance to ensure that your payments are always made. That can cost a couple of percent added to the principal amount of your loans. However, once again, thanks to a new idea, the amount of money needed inside your RRSP can shrink to only a few thousand dollars.

These are changing times. With high tax rates consumers are aiming more of their disposable income at tax-saving plans, especially the RRSP. In coming years the amount you can contribute will gradually rise to $15,500 per year. As a result, the number of RRSPs is about to balloon. However, it is still one of our cardinal rules that we try to pay down our non-tax-deductible loans as fast as possible, so why not combine the two?

One Canadian trust company has just introduced a new plan that will allow this to happen. I suspect, though, knowing the competitive nature of the financial services industry, that it won't be long before others are forced to follow. In the meantime this idea is only available through Firstline Trust.

Here's how it works. If you have a $50,000 mortgage with Firstline Trust (it could be one of several) and you contribute $3,000 to your RRSP, again with Firstline, they will use the $3,000 inside your plan to buy $3,000 of your mortgage. Now, when you make your monthly payments, part of the interest will go into your RRSP, and part will go to the trust company. The next time you make a contribution to your RRSP, more of your mortgage will be purchased by your RRSP. Eventually your entire mortgage will be owned by your RRSP, and from then on you will make payments to yourself rather than a commercial lender. In fact, if you took a $100,000 mortgage at today's rates and made the maximum contribution to your RRSP each year, you would own your own mortgage in only nine years. That's a powerful incentive by itself. In addition, though, is the advantage that you now have freed up an extra $100,000 in borrowing power that you can use elsewhere.

This idea always included so many fees that you needed a $30,000 to $50,000 RRSP before it was viable. Now, though, the small guy can do it because Firstline will pay for the NHA insurance and most of the administration fees. In fact, the only extra cost is a $20-a-month administration fee and a three-quarters-of-one-percent setup fee based on the amount of RRSP transferred to

Firstline. That means homeowners with only $3,000 or so in their RRSPs can now use this type of plan.

Consider this idea. You have a mortgage that's coming due for renewal and you also have a chunk of cash inside your RRSP. If you transfer your plan and your loan to this company, all the funds inside your RRSP will be credited toward your mortgage. Now when you make a payment, your RRSP earns the going mortgage rate rather than the lower GIC or term deposit rate that you probably earned before. If you switch employers and roll your pension into your RRSP, you'll have even more "mortgage" money at your disposal. If you retire and get a golden handshake you can do the same. And can you imagine having an extra few thousand dollars a year? Rather than struggling over whether you contribute to your RRSP or pay down your mortgage, you do both.

How long can it be until other companies follow suit?

70

Shorten Three-Year Spousal Rule

It's common knowledge that money contributed to a spousal RRSP must remain there for three years before it's withdrawn. Otherwise, the withdrawn monies will be taxed in the higher income spouse's name, and that defeats the purpose of a spousal RRSP.

When we contribute to a spousal RRSP, our thinking is that we, the higher-tax-bracket individual, will save on taxes, but our lower-taxed spouse will eventually pay the tax when the money is removed. That's great thinking, except that we must wait three full years after our last contribution before our spouse can remove it at his or her lower tax rate.

But that's not necessarily so. Through smart financial planning we can shorten that time frame substantially. You see, the three-year spousal RRSP rules are based on the calendar year. That means that the individual who contributes money to a spousal RRSP on the final day of February 1992 will get credit on his or her 1991 tax return. Because they have to wait until the first day of 1994 before they remove the money, they have really only kept their money in a spousal RRSP for 22 months rather than the required 36. As a result, they have faster cash flow plus some extra tax relief.

The choice of investments, though, may have some bearing on how well this idea works. If, for example, you choose a five-year term deposit inside your RRSP, you wouldn't be able to remove the money — even if you wanted to — before the five-year life of the term deposit has expired. As a result, if you want to put yourself in position to remove money from a spousal RRSP as early as 22 months from the last contribution, you should choose a short-term investment.

Who might want to take advantage of this idea? Well, young people for sure. It's not uncommon for young couples to experience work disruptions as they raise families. They could save taxes at a high rate by having the husband contribute money to a spousal RRSP — with the wife removing it as early as 22 months down the road when she leaves work to start a family.

Investors could also use this type of planning. If one spouse has salary or pension income and the other only investment income, this idea may work well. The working spouse can contribute to a spousal RRSP. The nonworking spouse could purchase investments that compounded for three years at a time. That way the nonworking spouse could earn investment income for two years and remove the money from his or her spousal RRSP in the third year. The tax savings when the working spouse makes the contribution will be large. The tax bill when the nonworking spouse removes the funds will be small. The family, as a whole, pockets the difference.

Actually, you needn't restrict this type of planning to only once in a lifetime. It can be used every few years if your planning is right.

71

Get an Extra $300 Tax Rebate on Your RRSP

Normally, Canadians wait until the very last minute to contribute money to their RRSPs. When we do that, though, we play right into the hands of the taxman.

We can no longer earn $1,000 in tax-free investment income. However, all income earned inside a registered retirement savings plan compounds completely free of tax as long as the money remains inside the plan. There are absolutely no restrictions on the amount of tax-free income we earn until age 72 when the money must be removed from our plan. Even then, though, we can transfer the funds into a registered retirement income fund where we will gradually withdraw the funds by age 90.

Recognizing that, everybody who earns any taxable investment income should make it a point to contribute to their RRSPs at the very beginning of the year rather than waiting until the final deadline. The income earned by the RRSP will be totally tax free until it starts to produce an income in your own name. That should be many years down the road, and will give you years of tax-free compounding inside your RRSP.

For example, the individual who contributes $7,500 to an RRSP at the beginning of the year rather than the end will earn $750 tax free inside the RRSP rather than earning it outside his or her plan where it would be taxable. For the average Canadian taxpayer that would create a tax savings of $262.50. For those in the higher tax brackets it could mean a saving of as much as $375 — which surely could be used elsewhere. The point is that those who earn taxable income would be better off if they contributed to the RRSPs at the start of the year rather than waiting until the normal deadline.

72

Benefits for the Young RRSP Holder

The term "registered retirement savings plan" can scare many young taxpayers away from using these plans because they are young and have no interest in thinking about retirement. That's a shame since an RRSP should primarily be looked on as a tax-saving device, a "rebate savings plan," by young taxpayers. I mean, why pay taxes when you have these plans that will legitimately save you tax dollars? At the same time, the money inside the plan will grow at a much faster rate because it's compounding tax free rather than continually being taxed when left in your own name.

Consider these numbers. If a 30 year old saves $1,000 a year in his or her own name and earns 8% per annum until age 65 the pool of money will total $40,000. Clearly, it's worthwhile. If, however, the very same person saved the very same amount for the very same period of time and earned an identical rate of return, but did so inside an RRSP, the pool of money would total $185,000. That's right, an additional $145,000 for no more money simply because you used a savings plan (SP) with an "R" in front of it (RSP).

Unfortunately, though, we regularly procrastinate. That costs us twice. In the first place we pay more tax than necessary, and secondly, our money doesn't work as long for us and doesn't compound as rapidly. For example, a 30 year old who contributed $3,000 a year to an RRSP each year until he or she turned age 65 would accumulate $705,373.83 if the yearly yield earned an average of 9% per annum.

However, had this same individual begun contributions only five years earlier at age 25, he or she would accumulate some $400,000 extra inside the RRSP even though there was only $15,000 (five years at $3,000) extra contributed. Where else could a young individual earn $400,000 so easily?

Clearly, it's extremely advantageous for a young person to start one of these plans as early as possible. In fact, if a 25 year old contributed only $1,000 a year to an RRSP each year until age 65 he or she would accumulate more than a 40 year old who contributed $3,000 a year until age 65.

There can be no question that the yield you earn is important, but so is the amount of time that the money can work for you. It's like an employee who's making a profit for you. The longer it happens the more you profit, even though you aren't doing the work.

A younger person can also benefit substantially by thinking and acting short term when it comes to RRSPs. For example, if you're working full time right now you're paying full-time taxes. If you plan to quit work to return to school, why not contribute the maximum to your RRSP while you are working? Save the tax rebates to pay for your tuition. Then, when you go back to school and your income falls you can remove the funds from your RRSP at a very low rate — if, in fact, you are taxable at all. At that time you'll have your tuition as a tax deduction, your standard deductions and the full-time student deduction. With these extra deductions and a lower income you can probably remove substantial sums of money from your RRSP tax free.

The same theory applies to anybody who is expecting their income levels to fall in coming years. If you are planning a family and expect to quit work to raise that family you can expect your income level to fall when you cease working. You will benefit by contributing the maximum to an RRSP now, when your income level is high, and removing the money later when your tax rate is lower — if, of course, you are taxable at all.

The other example I like to use is one that fits in perfectly right now. There are many Canadians with the entrepreneurial spirit. If you are working full time now but planning to start a business of your own an RRSP is a natural for you. You should contribute the maximum to your RRSP now when you will get substantial tax relief. When you start your company you can use the tax rebates you've been accumulating as seed money. Then when you need more money you can withdraw amounts of money equal to the tax deductions generated by your company completely tax free. From then on if you want more money you can also remove it from your RRSP at little, if any, tax. You see, a good accountant can probably arrange the affairs of a new company in such a way that you can earn tax-free income for the first two years. That will allow you to remove money virtually tax free from your RRSP.

Yes, I know that RRSPs are generally looked on as being valuable to older people and being for long-term retirement purposes. However, these examples show you that these plans are actually very valuable for young taxpayers and very useful in the short term.

73

Make RRSP Loans Tax Deductible

Prior to 1981, we used to able to borrow money to contribute to an RRSP and make the interest cost tax deductible. The 1981 budget ended that. However, all loans that were already in place can still be considered tax deductible with the interest cost creating tax relief as long as these loans are still in place. In addition, those who take out new loans to contribute to RRSPs can also make those loans tax deductible. It's simply a matter of arranging them properly.

For example: Let's say you have some stocks, bonds, CSBs or mutual funds in your name right now. You don't want to cash them in as you expect further appreciation in their value. But maybe you should. If you cashed them in and used the proceeds to contribute to your RRSP, you'd then be able to buy back the very same or different investments with borrowed money. That loan would be considered an investment loan — and the interest paid on investment loans is considered totally tax deductible.

In essence you've made your RRSP loan the equivalent of tax deductible.

When you cash these investments you may not be too excited about the prospects of paying commission. You may feel that selling one day and then buying right back with borrowed money will create a double commission that will eliminate the advantages of this tax-saving idea. Well, don't worry. When you sell investments in this way you don't necessarily have to use a broker or pay a commission. You can always sell the securities privately, use the proceeds for your RRSP contribution, and then borrow to buy them back. It will make your RRSP loan much easier to service.

74

How to Deduct Loans for RRSPs

In the near future Ottawa is expected to release new rules on interest deductibility. It's imperative, then, that each and every investor assess his or her outstanding investment loans. In fact, taxpayers should always do this once a year or so, as it's always advisable to pay off all non-tax-deductible loans before those that remain tax deductible. Then as cash becomes available, you will always know where to direct it.

One area of confusion has always involved loans taken to contribute to a registered retirement savings plan. These loans used to be tax deductible, but back in 1981 the rules were changed.

As I mentioned, any loans taken out to contribute to an RRSP, registered pension plan or income averaging annuity contract after November 12, 1981, are not tax deductible. As a result, they should be on the "hit list" of loans to be paid off as fast as possible. Loans taken out before that date were tax deductible and will continue to be so forever, unless the rules are changed. These loans should be at the bottom of the list when it comes to pay-down priority.

While spousal RRSP contributions are great when it comes to income splitting, any interest incurred when you borrow to contribute to a spousal RRSP is not and never was tax deductible. These loans should also be paid down as fast as possible.

Income averaging annuity contracts were very useful for athletes, entertainers and so forth before 1982. These people could use all their earnings to buy a "pension." They would then pay tax only as they earned the income. Any loan taken out to buy an IAAC was and still is tax deductible. These should be amongst the last loans paid off.

It is still possible to make an RRSP loan tax deductible, yet few of us take the time to arrange our affairs properly. For example, if you are able to claim your vehicle as a business deduction and you are planning to buy a new one, you'd be wise to take some of the cash you have available and contribute to your RRSP even if it means you have to finance more of your vehicle's purchase price. Borrowing for an RRSP contribution would not create a tax deduction, but borrowing for a business vehicle can.

This example doesn't always work. There are restrictions on the tax deductions we can claim when writing off vehicle expenses and loans, so make sure you have room in your vehicle limits before banking on this idea.

Likewise, any funds borrowed to run a business are tax deductible even though the business is not incorporated. Again, if you were in a position to borrow to run your business and free up cash to contribute to an RRSP or for any other non-tax-deductible use you'd be better off. Indirectly, you would have made your RRSP loan tax deductible.

Investors have the upper hand when it comes to RRSP contributions. They normally have monies invested outside their RRSPs. If you are in that position you have several alternatives. For example, if you want to contribute $5,000 to your RRSP and you have a like amount of money maturing in a non-sheltered investment, you simply liquidate the investment, contribute those funds to your RRSP and then borrow to buy another investment. Interest paid on investment loans is tax deductible provided you meet several requirements. The investment must produce a regular income and there must be some expectation of a future profit. If you meet these requirements you can generally expect once again, to have made your RRSP loan tax deductible in an indirect way.

Normally, we think of RRSPs in January and February. However, with possible changes to the interest deductibility rules and with recent tax changes, there's a valid reason to consider contributing earlier.

Generally speaking, changes to tax rules are not retroactive. Anything you legitimately put in place now should survive future changes. In addition, now that interest income is fully taxable it's advantageous to cash in interest-bearing investments as soon as possible and contribute to your RRSP. The earnings inside your RRSP are allowed to compound tax-free as long as they remain there. As a result, you win twice: you have less taxable income in your own name, and you have more income compounding tax-free inside your plan.

Let's not limit this discussion to RRSP loans. At this time we should assess all our loans with an eye to paying off all non-tax-deductible loans fast. Where possible we should also try to replace non-tax-deductible loans with those that are tax deductible.

75

RRSP Overcontribution Strategy

One of the new buzzwords in the registered retirement savings plan campaign is "overcontribution." New rules allow us to put an extra $8,000 into our RRSPs over and above the normal contribution limit. Yes, we get no tax deduction for this extra contribution. But, for some it can be valuable. In fact, financial planners, stock brokers, financial institutions and other RRSP issuers are swamped with requests for information on how to do it.

Here's the strategy. Canadians are lining up to make their final contributions to their RRSPs for last year. Tax saving contributions for 1991 must be in by the close of business April 29, 1992. This year though, it's easier to contribute for 1992 as well as we will be able to calculate our 1992 contribution limits once we know how much we earned in 1991. Yes, from now on our RRSP contributions are based on the previous year's income.

But, what if this is your first year working? What if you are a businessperson who had a bad year last year with no income but expect to earn a pile of money this year? And, what if you are retired and earn all your income from pensions and investment income? You don't qualify to use an RRSP as a tax deduction. But, you can still enjoy some of the long-term compounding available with an RRSP.

For the 1991 tax year Canadians are allowed to contribute up to $8,000 to an RRSP even though they get no tax deduction. Ottawa figured that Canadians would change jobs from time to time and mess up their RRSP limits so why not provide a buffer of sorts, an amount of money that could be in our plans from time to time without incurring any penalties even though it shouldn't be there. The financial industry has endorsed the strategy of "if it can be done, do it."

The real question is "why bother?" If you get no deduction why bother overcontributing?

Our strategy has been that you take every tax deduction you can get as often as possible since you will never get another chance. As a result, you should use your RRSP to the fullest when you get a tax deduction. Thereafter there is only value to overcontributing to an RRSP when you have used every other tax-saving device available. Yes, there is value to overcontributing, but, because it produces no tax relief it should be moved to the back burner until all the other tax-saving devices have been used. Things like tax shelters, leverage and charitable contributions will all produce tax savings and should be considered before overcontributing. In addition, some investments produce yields that are taxed at a lower rate. Included are Canadian dividends that qualify for the dividend tax credit. It can help many Canadians earn up to $22,000 a year in tax-free dividends. In addition, we are each entitled to earn up to $100,000 in tax-free capital gains in a lifetime by investing in assets that grow in value.

However, for some overcontributing can produce some exciting benefits. Consider individuals who do not like to invest in stocks or mutual funds. They are die-hard term-deposit-type investors. They sleep well at night knowing their money is safe. The problem they have is that interest income is totally taxable. If they can't contribute to an RRSP they can't enjoy tax-free compounding. Or, if the amount they can contribute is small, they don't enjoy much benefit. And, what about those who are able to contribute the maximum but still have lots of money that they wish to keep invested in guaranteed investment certificates? They will have to pay full tax on any interest they earn.

If they contributed $8,000 to an RRSP even though they got no tax relief, that money would compound tax free inside their plan rather than fully taxable outside. A 12% yield would double every six years rather than every 10 to 12 years outside an RRSP. That's the key right there. The money will grow much faster because it's inside a tax-free environment.

If that were the only consideration it would be easy to recommend that everybody overcontribute. Naturally, there is a glitch.

When you put the $8,000 into your RRSP you get no tax deduction. If you leave it there longer than three years you must repay tax when you remove it. As a result, you must go short term and give up a lifetime of tax-free compounding (not the usual RRSP strategy) or leave it in there longer than three years and enjoy long-term tax-free compounding. If you leave it longer than 10 or 15 years, depending on your yield, you will win anyway. The money gained through tax-free compounding will be greater than the tax you will pay on the removal of the $8,000 that wasn't tax deductible in the first place. That's the strategy the tax planners are promoting. Put the money in without tax relief. Leave it longer than 15 years of tax-free compounding and you are a winner.

It's possible to improve your lot a bit through planning. If you overcontribute $8,000 this year but claim it as the first $8,000 of next year's contribution, you can then top up next year's level to the maximum and add on another $8,000. Now you haven't exceeded the $8,000 lifetime maximum, but you've extended the three-year period that allows tax-free removal. Following this strategy each year until age 71 *may* allow you tax-free compounding, the fullest tax relief and the right to remove your $8,000 tax free after all.

76

RRIF Better Choice Than Annuity

While most Canadians choose to remove the money from their RRSPs via an annuity, or by outright cancellation of their plans, there's now a better choice. It's called a registered retirement income fund or RRIF for short.

Why is an RRIF better than the other choices? It offers more flexibility, lower tax rates, and the return of more of your money than you'd normally get. That's why.

Under the old laws, we were only allowed one RRIF in a lifetime. Now we can have as many as we want. We used to be restricted to a smaller monthly income than we could get with an annuity, but now we can pick whatever we want, without restriction. With an annuity we never got our money back, just a monthly income. With an RRIF we get back all our original money plus all the investment income earned inside the plan.

So, clearly, there's now much more flexibility with an RRIF than with an annuity. And, of course, when it comes to comparing the RRIF to the third option — that is, to collapse your RRSP outright and pay full tax — it's even more important to choose the RRIF. If you cash in, your pay full tax. If you choose the RRIF, you can spread the tax liability over 20 to 30 years. In fact, with proper tax planning you can actually get most or all of the money out of your RRIF totally tax free.

To show you how attractive these plans now are, consider these numbers. If you have a registered retirement savings plan and you go the annuity route at age 71 you'll receive almost $12,000 a year lifetime income. In addition, it's guaranteed to last at least 15 years in case you predecease your spouse. In 15 years, then, you will have received a little more than $177,000.

Unfortunately, though, because you've had no inflation protection, your income is now worth only 25 cents on the dollar.

Instead, you could choose an RRIF. If you were able to earn 15% on your money inside the plan while taking the very same income as you were going to from the annuity, you'd still have $218,000 inside your RRIF 15 years from now. It would continue to produce an income for the rest of your life and for the rest of your spouse's, and still leave a sizable amount for your heirs when both of you pass away.

With the annuity everything stops when you die, although in this case there is a 15-year guarantee. And, if you live, you have to recognize that inflation will gradually destroy the purchasing power of your fixed-income annuity.

If you chose the RRIF instead, you'd have the flexibility to increase your income to $15,000 after five years and, let's say, to $20,000 after another five years. And even while you're protecting yourself against inflation, you'd still have $120,000 left after 15 years. That will still earn a pretty healthy income for the rest of your years.

The new RRIF rule works very much in your favor, so make sure you consider them, as well as an annuity, when it comes time to remove the money from your RRSP.

77

Maturing CSBs

Huge numbers of Canadian taxpayers could feel a very painful tax bite this year if they don't act quickly. At the end of October each year the Bank of Canada pays out the yearly yield on Canada Savings Bonds to those who chose yearly interest payments. At the same time an issue or two matures. Holders of those bonds get back the original purchase price tax free (it's simply the return of their own money so it shouldn't be taxable) plus they may receive a large sum of money for past years' worth of compounding. This compounded money can produce a tax problem.

This fall a huge CSB issue, Series 39, purchased in 1984, matures. The Bank of Canada says there are $3.3 billion worth of these bonds outstanding. They will present no tax problem. However, the interest payable for 1991 alone is close to $400 million. Since the cancellation of the $1,000 tax-free interest deduction all interest is fully taxable. There is no way to avoid it unless you use other tax-saving strategies to offset this income.

The bigger problem, though, develops when taxpayers have been compounding their CSB or other interest. We used to be able to compound tax free as long as we wanted. We paid tax when we finally matured the investment. The maximum compounding period was reduced to three years a few years ago and has now been eliminated for investments purchased from January 1 onward. Some investors still own investments where there can be a balloon payment, with the accompanying balloon tax bill, at the end. Investments purchased prior to 1990 can still be compounded for three years. As a result, there can be some giant tax headaches created by this year's and next year's maturing Canada Savings Bond issues and by term deposits and guaranteed investment certificates.

There are some ways around this problem. If you qualify for a registered retirement savings plan but haven't used it, this should be the year. CSB and other interest-type income doesn't qualify for contribution to an RRSP. However, if you receive salary, alimony, real estate income or a golden handshake, you should do the necessary calculations to put extra of these types of income into your plan to offset the extra investment income you stand to earn this year. The interest will effectively become tax free and you will be able to compound it tax free inside your plan.

Some taxpayers would find this a hardship. They need the money and would not be able to leave it inside their RRSP for an extended period of time. In this case it's best to calculate how much you can get along without. Maybe you put half the money into your RRSP this year and then remove it at the turn of the year. You would lower your tax bracket this year and increase it next year. However, the average of the two years would normally be better than taking a big tax hit this year.

If you also have a large compounding investment coming due next year you may want to put as much as possible into your RRSP this year and next year. After two years you can start to remove the money from your plan as you need it.

In fact, if you look at what's been happening with our tax system you have to feel that income tax rates will eventually start to fall. The GST is a cash cow. It produces more money, money that is easily traceable, than even Ottawa expected. It will be easy in the future to increase the GST rate while reducing income tax rates. If you believe this to be true you should take every tax deduction you can now even if you intend to cancel it in the next few years. The tax you pay when you cancel will probably be less than the tax you saved in the first place. Plus you enjoy tax-free compounding inside the plan.

If you don't qualify for a registered retirement savings plan you may want to consider manufacturing an offsetting tax deduction by purchasing units in a tax shelter. The real estate markets are recovering from the effects of the recession. We should be able to manufacture some offsetting tax relief and also expect to earn tax-free capital gains down the road.

Some people quality for an RRSP even though they may not realize it. Pension income no longer qualifies for inclusion into your own RRSP. However, it can be contributed to a spousal plan if your spouse is under age 72 and if the pension income is from a work-related pension.

This might be the perfect answer. Take $6,000 of pension and put it into a spousal RRSP. This will offset $6,000 worth of interest. The money is now in your spouse's name. If he or she is in a lower tax bracket than you, the tax bill will be less when it is eventually removed three or more years down the road, or through an annuity or RRIF. You save taxes and practise income splitting at the same time.

78

The Golden Handshake: Make It Work

Have you lost your job? If you have you aren't alone. Or, have you been offered one of those early retirement packages? You know, where you get a nice fat golden handshake, or parachute, as it is called. If you are in either of these positions you have a potential tax problem that can be avoided.

When you leave a company one thing you have to look at is your pension. Because of recent changes many Canadians mistakenly believe they cannot roll any of their pension into their registered retirement savings plans. That is not true.

If your pension is being wound down or you are to receive a lump sum payout from your pension these amounts can still be rolled over directly to your RRSP. The trick is to ensure that you don't touch the money. The institution where you have your RRSP should be empowered to go after the pension funds. Now the money will transfer directly from your pension to your RRSP without any tax consequences. In fact, you don't even have to add the income to your tax return. It's simply a transfer from one trustee to another. Whatever you do, though, do not take this money yourself. If you do it will be considered normal income and only the normal 18% of your earned income to a maximum of $11,500 can be transferred into your plan. When you start drawing a pension don't forget that the first $1,000 will normally be tax free because of the pension income deduction. In addition, we are still allowed to transfer $6,000 per year of pension income into a spouse's RRSP until 1994.

If you've lost your job or been retired it's common to resist taking tax-saving steps as you figure you have less money to work with. However, if you keep sending money to Ottawa you are going to kiss it goodbye forever. Take the tax deductions now so you will still have the money invested inside your RRSP earning income. It will help produce income for a long period of time.

When it comes to the golden handshake it's extremely important that we learn to use the rules properly. Otherwise we can lose as much as half the funds.

When you get a departure settlement from your employer it's taxed as normal income. However, if you also work most of the year for this employer or a new one or if you receive salary plus pension plus a settlement you can be pushed sky high into a new tax bracket or two. Once again your RRSP can come to the rescue.

We are allowed to roll over up to $2,000 of settlement into our RRSPs for each year we worked for the company. If we worked any years prior to 1989 when we did not have a pension at work we can bump the roll-over amount up to $3,500 for those years. As a result, most employees who worked 20 years for a company could transfer $20,000 or more of a golden handshake into an RRSP.

It looks like this money will now be earned tax free. However, there is a possible glitch. It's called the alternative minimum tax. When we have an unusual jump in income in one year we can trigger the AMT even though we transferred this money into our RRSP. But, don't worry. If this is a one-time jump and your income levels back down in coming years you should be able to recoup the AMT you paid.

It may also be possible to ease the tax problem on settlements by talking to your employer. In some cases it might be possible to spread your settlement over this year and next. Now, you may not be bumped into such a high tax bracket and if you use the rollovers we've been mentioning you may not have to worry as much about the AMT. The drawback to this strategy is that you don't get your money as fast and won't be able to earn as much with it. You have to decide whether to take it all now or split it over two years, unless, of course, you can convince your employer to pay you interest between now and January when you receive the second installment. This may not be a big problem for your employer if you have been a valued employee.

Don't forget that he or she will have the use of your money throughout that time period.

Why roll this money into your RRSP if you are going to need some of it to live on? It's simple — to save taxes. If you put it in now you save being bumped into a higher bracket. Then the money earns tax-free income inside the plan. And, if you want money you can always remove it a bit at a time. If you remove $5,000 or less at a time the institution is required to withhold only 10%. Up to $15,000 it's 20% and beyond that it's 30%. Yes, you will have to add these amounts to your income and pay tax on them when you file your return. In the meantime, though, you would have been earning income on the remainder tax free inside the plan, plus you would have enjoyed the use of the difference between your normal tax rate and the lower amounts withheld by the institutions. In the long run you'll have a more prosperous retirement.

79

Life Insurance Can Even Pay Off While You're Alive

Most of us look on life insurance as something that will help our heirs when we die. However, there are ways to advantageously use our life insurance while we're alive, and get some tax relief at the same time.

For example, if you are borrowing money for investment or other purposes, and the lender wants the loan life insured, the premiums you pay will normally be tax deductible.

When we buy life insurance to protect our family, the premiums aren't normally tax deductible as we aren't looking to earn money with this policy — we're simply using it as protection. Revenue Canada demands that expenses we incur can only be tax deductible when they are undertaken for business purposes.

Ah, ha. But when we are ordered to buy life insurance to protect a loan or for business purposes then the premiums are, indeed, tax deductible.

Lots of lenders offer life insurance on loans anyway. In that case the premium is often incorporated in your monthly payment. If the interest is tax deductible so, too, is the insurance portion. In that case we don't have much problem. In the instance where we go out and get a separate policy, though, that's when we often forget to claim the insurance premiums as a business or investment expense.

When in doubt ask the agent, the financial planner or the lender.

80

Split Your Pension Income

As income tax rates increase it's more important than ever that we move as much money out of the higher-taxed spouse's name into the name of the lower-taxed one. That way any investment income earned by the family will at least be taxed at the lowest rate possible. The new rules make it more important than before because of the new "clawback" provision to tax back the family allowance and old age security payments, forcing many taxpayers to pay as much as 64 cents on the dollar back to Revenue Canada. If you add property taxes and excise taxes, sales taxes and sin taxes to that number, you could actually pay more than 100% tax.

If you receive or are about to receive Canada Pension Plan, consider splitting your CPP payments in half. If one spouse is in a substantially lower tax bracket, that spouse will pay less tax on your CPP payments than if you reported the entire amount. To make these arrangements you'll have to be in touch with a financial planner or Welfare Canada. Before you do, though, you should assess the value. If both spouses receive CPP you each must split your payments. If you receive equal amounts there's little value in this idea. However, if the lower-income spouse receives little or no CPP it's very much worth your while.

Many seniors manufacture their own money problems. The husband was often the worker while the wife raised the children. He earned the money, so he also accumulated the investments and other family assets. Now he earns all the investment income while she earns virtually none. He may also have an employer's pension plus CPP and Old Age Security payments. Let's say he's in the top tax bracket, that is, around 48%. That also mean he will lose much or all of his OAS. If he moves some of the assets to his wife, she will pay much less tax on the income, he will be able to keep his OAS and, in fact, they may be able to get away with paying no tax at all.

One way to do that until the end of the 1989 RRSP season was to put every penny possible into a spousal RRSP. However, if your have company pension, $6,000 of it can be rolled into your spouse's RRSP per year between now and 1994. If you aren't using an RRSP now, this tactic will save you a great deal of tax. You will get tax deductions at a high tax rate and earn tax-free income inside your spouse's RRSP that will eventually come out as pension income taxed at your spouse's lower tax rate. If you are using an RRSP you'll still win. You can contribute 20% of your earned income to either your RRSP or one in your spouse's name. The tax savings are the same in either case. However, when the money comes out it will be taxed at a lower rate in your spouse's name. In addition, the $6,000 of company pension you are allowed to contribute to an RRSP between 1991 and 1994 can only be contributed to a spousal RRSP.

It's also possible to transfer assets to the lower-income spouse and maybe pay no tax at all. You see, there are no taxes on capital gains until we exceed $100,000 in a lifetime. If all the investments are in the higher-income spouse's name, you'll pay more. But what about this idea? Let's say you own a principal residence. You're planning to sell it and move into a rental unit. If you invest all the money in the higher-income spouse's name, that spouse's net income and taxable income will rise substantially. Much of the investment income will be lost to the taxman.

Your principal residence is half yours, half your spouse's. When you sell it there's a justifiable reason for splitting the money 50-50. Some accountants say that when only one spouse earned money to pay for the house, the original purchase price should be given to that spouse with the remainder split equally. Whichever route you follow, today's real estate prices mean substantial profits to be invested in the lower-income spouse's name.

There's one other thing that seems to gaining approval. Let's say the husband owns a substantial chunk of investments. He's already used up a portion of his $100,000 capital gains exemption and seems sure to exceed the maximum tax-free level. At the same time his wife has no chance of earning any capital gains. Why not get a firm appraisal on the value of the investments? Then write a letter to your spouse giving her the right to buy your investments at today's face value anytime in the future. As long as she pays you a small amount of money and agrees to pay today's face value she could sell the investments someday in the future, give you today's value and claim the rest as a capital gain in her name. That way she earns tax-free capital gains rather than you paying tax on them.

81

Pensioners Can Earn Loads of Tax-Free Income

It's a shame, but it's commonplace for Canadians to direct most or all of their savings toward things like term deposits and Canada Savings Bonds as they get older.

The rationale is great. The older you get, the more secure you want your investments to be. And those investments are very secure. The problem, though, is that all the income produced by them is interest, and now all interest is taxable.

If, instead, you purchased something — say, cases of canned food that wouldn't spoil — and sold it off over the next few years you'd be able to create a regular income, and normally one that would rise in value. You see, inflation will push the price of those canned goods higher each year. The first money you get back will be your own. It, naturally, is tax free as it's simply the return of your own money. From then on you'll be earning a capital gain, which, under today's laws, is tax free until the $100,000 mark.

If you earn 10% a year interest, it's taxable. If you earn 10% capital gain through selling these products, it's tax free when it's within the maximum limits. The income is the same but the tax burden is much more attractive.

Most of us aren't into canned foods, though. But that's where something called a systematic withdrawal plan can be useful. Mutual fund companies invest your money. Each month they pay you an income. It's only the return of your money so it's tax free. In addition, they pay you some of the capital gains that are earned on the money. You have virtually tax-free income.

For example: I remember a case where a pensioner was selling his house to move into a rental unit. In the first place I recommended that he buy a condo so he would have the advantage of a tax-free principal residence. However, he decided he wanted a rental unit. If he invested the $100,000 (the money he was going to net out on his house sale) in term deposits he would earn about $12,000 a year. With the loss of the $1,000 tax-free investment income deduction he was going to pay full tax on all the income the term deposits paid. Yes, he could have tucked the money away in raw land, art or antiques that would have risen in value but he felt he wanted a monthly income from his investments to supplement his pension income. Rather than the interest-bearing investments, he could have invested his monies in a systematic withdrawal plan with a mutual fund company where he would have received the same amount of monthly income but paid much less tax. For example, Templeton Growth Fund would have paid him the same $1,000 a month but because it was really the return of his own money he would have paid much less tax. In fact, if he chose the term deposits he would have paid about $4,800 tax on his $12,000 interest income. If he chose the mutual fund he would have paid $173 in tax. The difference is close to $400 a month in after-tax income which surely would have added to his lifestyle. His other alternative, and a better one in my mind, was to reduce his monthly withdrawal plan to about $900 per month. The after-tax yield was still better than he would net from his interest-bearing investment. In addition, he wouldn't be attacking his mutual fund investments to the same extent so they would compound that much faster.

82

Savings Plans — Don't Forget Important Deductions

Canadians are big savers. However, we are also big losers when we don't take advantage of legitimate tax deductions that are allowed once we start to earn investment income. And don't think that investment income means the stock market or real estate. No sir. We're talking about things as elementary as savings accounts and Canada Savings Bonds.

The first consideration is safety. While many consumers may hide their cache of savings in the basement, most use safety deposit boxes. If you declare interest or other investment income on your tax return, you can deduct the cost of renting a safety deposit box. If you're into stocks and bonds, you may be charged a safekeeping charge by the financial institution or stockbroker. Or you may pay banking charges to have the securities delivered and cheques crossed. These charges are tax deductible. Commissions, per se, are not tax deductible, but it *is* important to calculate commissions because they will lower your capital gains.

Other deductions we should claim include portfolio management fees paid to a bank or trust company, accounting fees, bookkeeping fees, investment counselling fees and investment literature and courses and interest paid on investment loans. Many consumers buy Canada Savings Bonds on the payroll deduction or monthly savings plans. This is really a loan that you pay off over a 10-month period. The interest is normally calculated at the same rate as you earn on your CSBs. We must pay interest on every penny worth of interest we earn, so it's important that we claim the interest we pay on payroll deduction plans as a tax deduction. In fact, when we look at it closely it's this fact that will ensure that interest on investment loans remains tax deductible for many years. If we had to pay tax on our CSB interest but were refused deductibility on our payroll deduction costs, we would no longer buy CSBs on payroll deductions plans.

Your employer has information on the cost of buying these bonds on payroll deduction and will provide you with them whenever you ask.

The interest paid on any other investment loans should also be claimed as a tax deduction. After all, if all investment income is taxable to some degree it's important that we claim the expenses we incurred to earn these monies as a tax deduction. In essence, we are operating a business when we invest. Businesspeople get tax relief — so, too, should we.

83

Don't Use the Government as a Forced Savings Plan

Would you believe that millions of Canadians purposely use the tax return to create a larger than normal tax rebate each spring? Here's what they do. They purposely leave a dependant or two off the exemption list they file with their employer each new year. In fact, some who are married go as far as to claim themselves as single.

Why? Well, their thinking is that there will be more taxes deducted from their paycheque all year long. But when they file their tax returns each spring, they'll claim the spouse and/or children that they've had all along. Now they'll get a much bigger tax rebate which they can use to finance a summer vacation. For some, the money may be used more constructively, such as to buy investments, pay off debts, or pay down a mortgage. Those are all great ideas and well worthwhile, but to save the money this way is a mistake.

All you're really doing is playing into Revenue Canada's hands. Your employer is obliged to remit these excess taxes to Ottawa every two weeks. That means that Revenue Canada has your money from mid-January right through until the day you receive your tax rebate. That can be 15 to 16 months down the road.

Surely you could have used that money to your own advantage in that time period!

Many taxpayers respond that it's the only way they can save money. It automatically disappears from their paycheques so they can't spend it until they get their rebate cheques in the mail.

Well, that's not really the case, you know. There are lots of other ways to set up a forced savings plan that will accomplish the same thing.

For example, why not continue to use Ottawa to provide your forced savings plans? But make it a different agency where you get paid interest rather than lose it. Each November Ottawa sells billions of dollars worth of Canada Savings Bonds. In many cases your employer will automatically deduct money from your paycheque to buy these bonds from the Bank of Canada. There's your forced savings plan. But instead of your earning no interest on the money that prematurely goes to Revenue Canada, this money earns the going CSB rate of interest. In addition, you have more flexibility. You see, you cannot retrieve your tax rebate until you file your tax return. CSBs can be cashed any time you want.

Another idea would be to have your paycheque automatically deposited in a savings account at a financial institution. Then you would authorize the manager to remove an agreed upon amount from the savings account each pay. Once again you have a forced savings plan that earns you a little something during the year.

Or what about increasing the size of your mortgage payment? And if you switch to a weekly mortgage with a larger payment, you can automatically pay your mortgage off in close to half the normal time. Or what about a monthly purchase of stocks, mutual funds or even a registered retirement savings plan?

Don't let your employer withhold too many taxes from your paycheque. It costs you in the long run.

84

Dividend Reinvestment Programs

Without question, most investors can trace their greatest investment successes to forced savings plans, that is, entering into an obligation to steadily and regularly buy or pay for investments.

A house is the best example. Few of us can afford to pay cash for a house. Instead, we scrape up a down payment and force ourselves to make monthly payments until the loan is paid off and we own the property lock, stock and barrel. We may find a little money from time to time to accelerate the mortgage paydown, but it was the constant, systematic payment plan that made it work.

Some people refer to this theory as a forced savings plan; some look at it as dollar cost averaging. It can be used with housing, systematic purchase of stocks, mutual funds and other investments — and it's growing in popularity with small- and medium-scale investors who already own investments that produce a regular yield.

You see, if you have enough money to buy investments you probably don't need the yield, unless, of course, you have retired and use the investment income you earn to supplement your pensions. If you don't need the yield, yet take it, you will pay tax in most cases, and may incur commissions and other expenses to reinvest those funds. However, there is a way to ease some of these burdens. It's called a DRIP — a dividend reinvestment program.

These programs have long been offered by mutual fund companies and now are being introduced by a growing number of Canadian corporations. They make and save money for the investor and they provide a constant source of income for the corporation.

Here's how they work. If you presently own shares of a mutual fund or a dividend-paying corporation you receive dividends several times a year. If you take the dividends you pay tax on them (if you are taxable) and then spend the money or reinvest it. If you reinvest it in shares of that fund or company, or another one, you probably pay commissions when the purchase is made.

However, more than 100 companies and many of the mutual funds now allow existing shareholders to automatically reinvest those dividends right back into more shares commission free. If you like the company where you are dealing this is a nice way to save some costs and continually accumulate a larger holding. If you don't need the yield you are earning why take it? Why not reinvest it somewhere? If you like the company in which you are presently investing why not stick with it?

Saving commission costs is only part of the story. Many of the companies that offer dividend reinvestment plans also offer investors the right to buy additional shares at reduced cost. They recognize that a constant flow of new money reduces their need to borrow money or issue new share offerings.

For example, many companies allow investors to purchase shares with their dividends and also to buy enough additional shares to reach the next board lot (usually in multiples of 100 shares). Or, they may allow you to buy a set percentage of the shares that you already own. Effectively, by owning shares of that company you've been encouraged to buy more because they're commission free. There can also be an added bonus. Many companies actually reduce the price of their shares to existing shareholders who wish to add to their dividend reinvestment plans. There are numerous examples of companies that are happy to lower the purchase price of their shares by 5% and charge no commissions in this instance. Investors who use these accelerated purchase plans can get even cheaper exposure to their favorite investments.

Those who wish to "time" the markets, that is, buy when prices are low and sell when they are high, don't really like these purchase plans, since systematic investment means constant buying no matter what the price is. However, few ordinary investors are successful at buying at the bottom and selling at the top. As a result, the success ratio for ordinary investors is overwhelmingly in favor of systematic purchase plans.

There is some confusion as to the tax status of dividend reinvestment plans. If you own shares of Bell Canada, for example, you can invest your dividends in new Bell shares. Those dividends, though, must be claimed on your tax return as taxable income. Simply put, even though you didn't actually receive the dividends it's considered that you did, and that you subsequently sent them back to the company to buy new shares. However, if you receive Canadian dividends you are still entitled to claim the dividend tax credit to eliminate most or all of the tax on those dividends.

Not all companies offer these plans. Even when a company does it might not be advantageous to enroll. The best choices are ones that consistently pay a good yield and regularly increase their dividends. Included are banks, utilities and steel companies.

85

Make Sure You Borrow for the Right Purposes

Far too often, we make the mistake of borrowing for the wrong things. As an example, we own some Canada Savings Bonds and we're considering buying a car. If we borrow money to buy the car, the interest won't be tax deductible unless we use the car for business purposes. Yet, interest on loans taken for investment or business purposes is, in fact, tax deductible. Realizing this, we'd be better off cashing in our bonds to pay cash for the car and then borrowing money to buy new bonds or other investments. Now the interest on that loan is tax deductible and part of it is picked up by the taxman.

The reverse has an individual using cash to buy business equipment, parts, supplies or, again, a car. The interest we pay on loans taken out for business purposes is tax deductible, even if it's only a part-time business. In this case we'd be better off borrowing for all these things while we pay cash for our vacations, personal use items, mortgages and any other item where interest would not be tax deductible. We may actually get another bonus here in that business and investment losses can be used to lower our taxable income from salary or investments. As a result, the taxman may pay part of the interest and give us back some of the taxes we already paid.

We now have tax rules called CNIL (cumulative net investment loss), rules that make it more beneficial to claim business losses incurred when we are actually operating a business before we claim investment losses. As a result, it's better to borrow for business reasons first, investment purposes second and personal uses last.

86

A Loan Can Unite the Family

We used to be able to save taxes by splitting the family assets between spouses and even other family members. Ottawa did its best to eliminate income splitting from our bag of tax saving tricks. Now we have to work a little harder to accomplish it. It's still worthwhile, though, as any time we can shift income from a high-level taxpayer to one in a lower tax bracket, the family will save taxes.

One way to accomplish that is to arrange for the lower-income spouse to borrow money for investment purposes. The higher-income spouse may have to guarantee the loan. However, lodging the investments that are purchased as collateral may be all that is necessary.

The next step is to pay the interest. To accomplish that, the higher-income spouse can give enough money each month to the lower-income spouse. If the lower-income spouse were to invest this money the income earned would be taxable on the donor's tax return. But the lower-income spouse doesn't intend to invest the money. It's going to be used to service the debt on an investment loan.

The net result, hopefully, is that the investment will produce a higher rate of return than the interest expense. The difference will accumulate in the lower-income spouse's name, which is exactly what we are trying to accomplish.

In the early years, in fact, the lower-income spouse may not even be lost as a dependant exemption. The interest is tax deductible before calculating net income. As a result, it's only the income earned after deducting expenses that will be taxable and used in determining dependant status. In addition, if the lower-income spouse chooses stocks or mutual funds, the income can be part capital gain and part dividends where very little tax is payable. If it's real estate, there will be a capital gain plus rental income that can be offset by expenses.

87

If You Borrow Against a Life Insurance Policy, Try to Make It Tax Deductible

Taxpayers who own cash value life insurance policies normally know that they can lodge them as collateral if they need to borrow money. However, far too often they don't realize that they have value in the policy itself that they could use to their advantage.

Often the insurance company will lend them most of the built-up cash surrender value, and normally at an interest rate below that offered by most lenders. In fact, if you have an old life insurance policy taken out in the 1960s or earlier, you have the right to borrow at rates as low as 5% and 6%.

There's an extra advantage, though, when you borrow that money to invest elsewhere. The interest we pay on most investment and business loans is tax deductible. And as 5% and 6% loans are scarce as it is, a *tax-deductible* 5% or 6% loan is even better.

That's why we want to make the best possible use out of this type of loan. Sure, we can borrow from a policy and pay for our next trip, and yes, the cost would be a little lower because of the lower interest rate. However, borrowing from a life insurance policy for investment purposes would be even better. Then a 6% loan would cost only 3.6% for somebody in the 40% tax bracket, a 5% loan only 3% after tax.

When you borrow against a life insurance policy in this way it looks pretty simple. Borrow at 5% or 6% and earn twice as much. However, it's not quite that simple. In the first place bookkeeping is important. If you don't bother to declare the interest you paid you don't get a tax deduction. If you don't bother to invest the money properly you won't earn as much as you should. And, if you borrow too much you can be taxed.

Here's what can happen. If you borrow more than your adjusted cost base you are not just getting back your own money, you are making a profit. As a result, it's important that you have your financial planner or insurance agent assess the value of your policy before you borrow the entire cash surrender value. It's great to get a low-cost loan but it's not so great to pay tax on your own money. Once you borrow more than this policy cost you could pay tax on your profits.

88

A Loan from Your Boss May Be Tax Free

In the past it was a great idea to borrow money from your employer at little or no interest cost. You could buy a bigger and more expensive house without having to pay a larger mortgage payment.

Well, Revenue Canada didn't care for this idea. They felt that you were getting a tax-free benefit from your employer. As a result, they made some substantial changes to the rules. However, it can still be beneficial to get a low-cost loan from your employer. First of all, what qualifies as a loan? Well, if your employer lends you money or arranges for you to be able to borrow it at a beneficial rate, or offers the same conditions to a family member (e.g., a student for tuition purposes), you are considered to have received a benefit.

If you borrowed $10,000 from your employer at 4% and the government-set "prescribed rate" (usually set every quarter by the federal government — and usually the rate they pay us on late tax rebate cheques) averaged 10% all year you would have received a benefit of $600 (10% less 4% times $10,000). You would be required to claim the $600 as a taxable benefit on your tax return, prorated, of course, to cover the portion of the year the loan was outstanding. Even then, though, it's a cheap way to get a loan. But there are ways where it can be even cheaper.

If you borrow money from your employer to buy a new house, the prescribed interest rate that determines your taxable benefit is deemed to be the lesser of the rate in vogue at the time you made the loan and at present. Accordingly, it pays to take a short-term loan when it looks like rates are going to fall since your taxable benefit will gradually fall as rates fall. All you have to do is renegotiate your loan every quarter. If, however, it looks like rates are going to rise you won't want to change the terms of your loan.

If you are relocated by your employer, are required to buy a new house and can claim moving expenses as a tax deduction, you can get a break on the first $25,000 worth of housing loans received from your employer. Effectively, you do not have to include as a taxable benefit the gain you enjoyed on up to $25,000 in home relocation loans. You can enjoy this benefit for as long as five years.

Naturally, if you borrow money from your employer at the going rate or higher you do not have to worry about claiming any taxable benefit since you have not gained any advantage.

Many employees are encouraged to borrow money to buy shares of the company where they work. It improves employee relations. You own shares of the company so you prosper as it does. As a result, you may actually become more productive.

If you borrow money from a normal financial institution to buy shares of any company including the one where you work you can claim the interest as a tax deduction. Accordingly, the same theory applies to loans from your employer to buy shares in the company where you work. In this case the interest will be tax deductible as it is an investment loan. That tax deduction will offset the tax on the taxable benefit you claim on the lower cost of the employee loan. You own shares in your company and the tax cost is offset by the tax breaks.

The advantages offered by employee loans are not as attractive as they used to be. However, employee loans are still generally advantageous.

If you can borrow at a lower rate than you would pay at a financial institution and only pay your tax rate on a portion of the taxable benefit you have a pretty good chance of coming out ahead. In addition, if you believe in the company where you work you will probably benefit in the long run by owning shares in that company.

89

It Doesn't Pay to Cash Some Old Loans

While we should always try to pay off all non-tax-deductible loans as fast as possible, we don't have to act as quickly when it comes to investment loans as they *are* tax deductible.

There is one type of loan that creates extra confusion. It appears not to be tax deductible but in many cases it is. If it weren't tax deductible, it should be paid off as soon as possible. However, if it is tax deductible, it's better to put it at the bottom of the list — and pay it off last.

The loan in question is an old RRSP loan. Until 1981, we were allowed to claim the interest we paid on RRSP loans as a tax deduction. Since then, no such luck on new loans.

The point is, though, that these loans should not be paid off ahead of non-tax-deductible loans like mortgages and credit card balances because the interest on these tax-deductible RRSP loans is much lower than on a non-tax-deductible loan.

You should segregate any old RRSP loans from your other loans. In addition, you should continue to separate your tax-deductible loans from non-tax-deductible ones.

The order of payment should be against non-tax-deductible loans, then tax-deductible ones — and finally those that were originally taken out for RRSP contributions when these loans were still tax deductible. While interest rates should still play a role, the thinking here is that a typical investment loan can always be replaced by a new one down the road. Once the old RRSP loan is paid off, it can never be replaced.

90

Pay Cash for Gold, Raw Land

There's always been a great deal of controversy over which investment loans are tax deductible and which aren't. The courts seem to have made up their minds recently, though — and here's what they said.

To make interest on investment loans tax deductible, we must meet two requirements. The first is that we must earn a regular yield when we invest the money; the second is that there must be some potential for future profit. We can create all the losses we want along the way as long as we earn some kind of regular yield and as long as we can show Revenue Canada that there's a reasonable expectation of a profit sometime in the future.

Gold might be one investment that consumers should consider borrowing for. It shows the potential for future profit, but that's the only way you make money with gold — you sell it at a higher price. Revenue Canada has now determined that we cannot claim the interest we pay on loans taken out to purchase gold as a tax deduction. There are other ways to play the gold game where the interest is tax deductible. You could buy shares in a producing gold mine, a gold fund or a mutual fund with exposure to gold or shares of gold producers.

We have the same problem with raw land. Unless it's producing an income, the interest won't be tax deductible unless we're in the business of developing land. Of course, if we are we'll have to add the income we earn when we sell the land to our other income and pay full tax on it rather than earn a tax-free capital gain when we're simply an investor.

There are other ways to get involved in the real estate markets where the interest we pay can be tax deductible. Included are real estate trusts, shares of real estate companies, rental properties, farms, Christmas tree farms — or, at least, pick raw land that can be farmed, used as parking lots, or used in some other way to produce an income. That way the interest we pay is tax deductible so we save taxes while waiting for future profits.

When we buy investments it's best to buy ones that are multi-dimensional in scope. That is, they produce an income on a regular basis so we have some help in maintaining that investment throughout the years. At the same time they produce the potential for a capital gain. When we borrow for investment purposes it's even more important that there is some regular yield to help us pay the interest and other carrying charges while we wait for a capital gain. It's that combination of yields that also gives us the right to claim tax deductions.

91

Stock, Mutual Fund and Real Estate Commissions Aren't Tax Deductible — or Are They?

Normally we think that commissions paid to buy real estate, stocks or mutual funds are not tax deductible. However, they can be if we manage our money properly.

Normally, commissions aren't claimed as a business expense. Instead, they're added to the cost of the property or subtracted from the proceeds of a sale. That lowers the capital gain effectively giving us some tax relief on the commissions we pay.

But capital gains are now tax free, to $100,000 each in a lifetime. Some taxpayers, though, will exceed the yearly — and lifetime — limits. In that case, it's really important that we continue to claim our commissions when calculating our capital gains. In addition, a portion of our capital gains must be added to our normal income when we calculate the new minimum tax. So even though capital gains are tax free, they are in fact part taxable. Claiming commission expenses, then, can save some of these potential tax bills.

When you calculate your capital gains you should take your total out-of-pocket cost and subtract it from your net after expenses and commissions receipts. That way the capital gain you claim is the "pure" capital gain, the amount received after expenses. You'll erode your tax-free capital gains slower and pay less minimum tax. As a result, your commissions will be partially tax deductible. Once you exceed $100,000, they definitely are.

92

Real Estate Income Isn't Always Taxable

For some reason or other there seems to be great confusion over how to treat mortgage interest when you own two pieces of real estate. Handle it properly and you get tax-deductible interest expense. Make a mistake and you pay not only today's high interest rates but also get refused interest deductibility.

Here's what seems to be happening. Canadians who have paid off their mortgages or built a substantial amount of paid-up equity in their homes are buying a second property. It stands to reason that if you own two houses and borrowed money to produce rental income that the interest will be tax deductible. And, it can be — but only when handled properly.

For example: If you own a house in which you presently live and you borrow money against it to buy another house that you intend to rent you won't have much trouble with Revenue Canada. You see, in their eyes you have borrowed money to make money. They expect to share in your profits sometime down the road so they will generally accept your idea.

To make the interest on a loan tax deductible Revenue Canada demands that the investment you purchase produce a regular income *and* some expectation of a future profit. Rental real estate generally meets both requirements. If it's already constructed it should produce rental income and normally real estate rises in value. By the way, the rents do not have to exceed the cost of operation. In fact, that's one of the great advantages of real estate. If you finance it properly it can manufacture tax deductions that will save you taxes owing on other types of income.

Here's where problems develop, though. Many taxpayers believe they can buy a new home in which to live, rent out the existing home and still claim the interest as a tax deduction. In some cases it works but in most it does not. Let's examine what they've done. They live in a house that's paid for in full. They have great equity on which to borrow, so they do. But then they make the critical mistake. They use the money they raise to buy a house in which they plan to live. There's all kinds of hope for it to turn a future profit. But there's no hope of a regular income as they intend to live in the new house, not rent it out. It matters not that they intend to rent out their original house. They borrowed the money for house number two — and there will be no income generated by that house.

If interest deductibility is important they should handle this transaction differently. They could stay in house number one, borrow to buy house number two, rent it, and they have no problems (other than those created by being a landlord). They could sell house number one, use the proceeds to buy house number two in which they live and then use it as collateral to purchase house number three, which they rent. Now, the money was borrowed to produce rental income and a potential profit — and Revenue Canada should be happy.

There's also one other idea that could prove interesting. If you really want to hang onto property number one and also get interest deductibility, you could sell house number one to a friend, buy house number two, in which you plan to live, for cash, and then borrow against it to repurchase house number one from your friend. Now you own the two properties you originally desired and you have interest deductibility.

There are two problems with this final idea. The first is the fees it will attract. You may be able to negotiate with a lawyer and you won't need a real estate agent. However, you will have to face up to land-transfer taxes and other closing fees. In fact, you may have to pay them twice.

In addition, you may also attract the attention of Revenue Canada. As part of tax reform Michael Wilson has implanted some bicuspids into the tax avoidance rules. If Revenue Canada feels you have done something purely to create tax deductions they can refuse to accept that transaction.

Your lawyer and real estate agent can be a big help in making sure these transactions are handled properly and with the least expense. I mean, if you go ahead and borrow against house number one to buy house number two, in which you plan to live, it might take three years for Revenue Canada to spot the error. All of a sudden you may be responsible for three year's taxes on all the interest you claimed. It's better to do it right in the first place.

93

When Planning, It Pays to Look to the Outskirts

If you are earning taxable investment income that you don't need, it hardly makes sense to earn more. It only increases your tax burden.

Instead, why not buy a piece of property on the outskirts of town and let its value rise over the years? The gain is tax free until you sell it and even then it will be treated as a tax-free capital gain as long as you are under the $100,000 limit.

In fact, this is a tactic that should be practised by homeowners who may want to move elsewhere sometime in the future. You should look for a piece of property on the outskirts of town where you might want to live.

If you buy it at a decent price now you can enjoy double inflation protection. The value of your present house will rise, offsetting inflation, while you will also enjoy protection against inflation on your new property. As the city or town where you live expands, your property will rise in value. When it comes time to build you have several options: you can sell your house and build on the new property; you can sell both properties and move to another one; or you can work a swap deal with the builder whereby he buys your house and builds on your property or another one.

You come out with double inflation protection and can save transfer taxes, real estate commissions and capital gains taxes.

94

Buy a Hobby Farm

I know. We hear that the lot of Canadians farmers is not a happy one — that it's hard to make a profit. But, now that interest rates are falling maybe it's time for many Canadians to buy a farm, if only to save taxes.

When interest rates rose the real estate markets dove. Real estate tax shelters that were supposed to provide tax relief and capital gains when they were sold couldn't be given away. But, now that the opposite is happening, now that interest rates are falling, we have to expect real estate prices to rise.

One way to take advantage is to buy a farm. Now, some of us love to live on a farm and operate it full time. Others wouldn't want to leave the comfort of the city and, heaven forbid, soil their hands. Both individuals, though, can gain some tax relief.

Full-time farmers can use the "cash method" of accounting. As a result, they can manufacture operating expenses near the end of the year to lower or eliminate taxes owing on their profits. These rules were tightened considerably in the 1989 federal budget; however, they are still valuable.

I think there's a great opportunity for those taxpayers who don't want to be full-time farmers. They can buy land at bargain prices now that will certainly rise in price in coming years. And, they can manufacture tax relief along the way that will help them pay for this property. In addition, when they decide to sell it they will get tax relief. In some cases the gains will qualify for the $100,000 tax-free capital gains provisions. In some cases they may even qualify for the $500,000 limit. And, even if they are taxable, capital gains are taxed at a reduced rate.

The best example is a Christmas tree farm. Pick a spot outside of town where land is cheap. But, don't forget to look at the municipal growth patterns. It would be a nice bonus to own a piece of property that was paying its way that also jumped dramatically in value when it was needed for expansion.

If you operate a legitimate farming operation you are allowed to claim some startup expenses as tax deductions rather than capital expenditures. Included are the costs of clearing and levelling the land, installing drainage and even drilling wells so that you can provide irrigation. The normal operating expenses will also be acceptable. Things like interest on any mortgages and operating loans, maintenance costs, property taxes, tools, utilities, insurance premiums, even some vehicle expenses are all expenses that can be used to offset the income generated by the farm products sold.

But, what if you don't sell any products? After all, if you start a Christmas tree farm you can't expect to sell much product for seven or eight years. In this case some of these expenses can flow through to your tax return and be used to offset tax on your other forms of income.

Provided your farm shows a reasonable expectation of eventually producing a profit you have a reasonable argument when dealing with Revenue Canada. Take pictures at Christmas time. It's a major holiday. Everybody buys a Christmas tree. Prepare a fair operating plan. Agriculture agencies can help you in projecting when a normal crop of Christmas trees would come on stream. If you operate this farm the way you would operate any other legitimate business you shouldn't have any problems.

So, how much can you write off? Well, for the full-time farmer it's almost everything. It is difficult, though, to build inventory as the year ends and hope to use it as an immediate tax deduction. If you are a part-time farmer you compare your expenses to your farming income. The first $2,500 is a direct tax deduction against all other forms of income like salary, interest and pension income. In addition, you are entitled to claim one-half of the next $12,500 in expenses as a tax deduction against other forms of income. As a result, the taxman will allow you to earn all the farming income tax free plus up to another $8,750 in other income.

There's one more extremely attractive consideration. One of the operating expenses we can claim is labor. If you pay your spouse or children to work on this farm it's no different than if you hired a stranger. As long as the salaries paid are similar to those you would pay a stranger you have no problem. If your children have no summer job you can pay them to work on your farm. You claim the cost as a tax deduction. If the farm produces a loss it can be claimed as a deduction against other forms of income. The student now uses the income he or she earned to pay university tuition. Indirectly you have made your child's tuition tax deductible on your tax return. In fact, you can even manufacture a double tax deduction because part of a student's tuition costs can be claimed on a parent's tax return if the student doesn't need it.

Rather than claim these expenses as farming losses some accountants recommend you claim this operation as a forestry business. As a result, you don't have to worry about the restricted farm-loss rules. However, the downside is that your gains won't qualify for the $500,000 tax-free capital gains deduction and you won't have the ability to transfer your farm tax free to your heirs. Either way, though, a tree farm can produce tax relief and future profits.

95

If You Need Money But Don't Want to Sell Stocks, Try This Idea

If you're an active investor who keeps your money working much of the time, there may be the odd occasion when you want some money but you don't want to sell your investments, because you naturally expect them to increase in value.

When that happens, you have an easy way to raise cash. Simply take the investments to a lender, lodge them as collateral and borrow money for a short period until you either don't need it any longer or until your investments look like they are topping out and can be sold.

If you don't like the idea of borrowing money, you have another alternative. If you have a self-directed RRSP you can always sell your personal investments to the RRSP and remove an equivalent amount of money from the plan. The assets inside your plan can be invested in a variety of ways including stocks, bonds, mortgages, term deposits and mutual funds. If you have one of those you simply arrange to sell it to your RRSP. You can do whatever you want with the cash after that.

If you sell at a profit you might trigger a capital gain in your name, but that shouldn't be a problem if you haven't exceeded the tax-free limits.

If you own a term deposit or GIC that won't mature for a couple of years, this can be the perfect way to get your hands on the money faster than normal. Simply sell the term deposit to your RRSP now. You get the cash while the term deposit remains in effect, but inside you RRSP.

96

Leverage Can Help Save Taxes and Create Wealth at the Same Time

Leveraged investments became almost a buzzword in the financial community as interest rates tumbled. But really, they aren't new at all.

Leveraging means borrowing money to invest. For most of us it's the only way we can buy our homes. We lodge a downpayment and borrow the lion's share of the cost of the property. Then we make monthly payments until the loan is paid off. In the meantime, though, we expect the value of the property to rise — not just the part that's paid for, but the entire value. As a result, we stand to make substantially more through owning a property this way than if we purchased only what we could pay cash for.

The same theory has been proven successful in buying rental properties. If you pay cash for rental real estate, you'll earn more rental income than you have expenses to run the business. As a result, you'll have both positive rental income plus the expectation of a capital gain, which would be tax free under the $100,000 limit.

However, if you borrowed you could buy a much more expensive property. As a result, you'd be in position to reap a much bigger capital gain if the property rose in value. The "if" is not a very large one as real estate generally rises in value over a reasonable period of time.

In addition to the expectation of a larger than normal capital gain, you can also create immediate tax deductions. If the rental income is less than the cost of running the property, the excess can be claimed as a deduction against all other forms of income. Recognizing this, many investors purposely borrow enough to make the property create a loss. They are in position to earn what could be tax-free capital gains, the tenants pay for much of the cost of ownership, and they get a "manufactured" tax deduction against their other forms of income.

97

Leveraging with Mutual Funds Can Be Easier than with Real Estate

In recent years the idea of combining leverage with the purchase of mutual funds has become quite popular. It's more convenient than leveraging rental real estate in that you don't have to spend time managing the money. It's handled by the portfolio manager while you will normally be the landlord when you buy real estate.

The vulnerability can and cannot be greater with mutual funds. They move in tandem with the stock markets. As a result, when stock prices fall, so too can mutual funds. If you've purchased them with borrowed money, your down payment can be wiped out very quickly.

However, when held for a reasonable period of time (five, seven, ten years at least), leverage with mutual funds almost always pays off. For example: If you borrow to buy $50,000 worth of mutual funds and you pay 12% interest on your loan, you'll pay $6,000 a year interest. That interest is definitely still tax deductible. However, it must be claimed in a certain way thanks to tax reform. First of all it must be claimed against the interest income you earn. That's great because now that all interest is taxable this interest deduction will make our interest tax free.

The next thing we claim our interest expense against is our dividend income. Once again it is taxable. But, again we can make it tax free. In this case, though, we gain a tremendous advantage in that Canadian dividends from stocks and mutual funds qualify for the dividend tax credit. It is a tax-free rebate of taxes already paid or about to be paid. We get a double dip here in that we've now made our dividends tax free *and* we also get a tax-free tax rebate.

The third income against which we must claim this interest expense is any capital gains we earn. That's great if we've already exceeded our $100,000 in tax-free capital gains as we now make an additional gains tax free. If, however, we have not yet triggered $100,000 in tax-free capital gains it appears that we now must offset these gains against our interest expense. Effectively, it appears that our capital gains are now taxable. It's not quite that bad, in that any capital gains offset in this way do not have to be used as part of our $100,000 in tax-free capital gains. In actual fact what that does is extend our tax-free capital gains beyond the $100,000 tax-free level. The gains we made were offset by interest expense. The new gains qualify for the $100,000 tax-free capital gains exemption.

What you've done is create a tax break similar to what you received when you borrowed to invest in rental real estate. A tax deduction on one hand plus tax-free income on the other — and the opportunity to earn substantially higher returns because you own more funds.

The bonus advantage is that mutual funds can be sold on a minute's notice any business day while real estate can be difficult to unload in a bad market.

98

Leveraging Will Save Taxes but Don't Let It Cost You Money

While leveraging real estate, mutual funds, the stock markets or any other investment can pay off handsomely, it must be done properly or it can cost you dearly.

First off, to make an investment loan tax deductible you must invest in something that pays a regular income *and* creates the possibility of earning a future profit. In other words, it can lose money now and for a reasonable period of time provided the investment produces some sort of regular income and the prospects of a profit some time in the future.

As a result, borrowing to buy gold or raw land or antiques that aren't used in business could be a mistake. The interest wouldn't be tax deductible. Yes, the gain would be a tax-free capital gain up to the normal limits, but the theory behind leveraging is to produce a tax deduction plus a tax-free gain.

The second problem can occur through misuse of leveraging. When you borrow money to invest it's great when the investment rises in value. However, if the investment loses value you can lose money faster than normal. As a result, you must be able to continue servicing your loans without selling off your portfolio. That means that entering into a leveraging program should only be done when you feel without much question that you can continue to pay the interest on your loans for a reasonable period of time.

That's easy to do. Simply compare your income to your expenses. Whatever income you have in excess of expenses that you think you'll have for a reasonable number of years, you can use to service a leverage loan.

That way, if the markets turn downward for a few months or a year, you won't have to sell your investments. If you simply borrow hoping that the investment will service itself, you may have to sell some of the investment to service the loan right when the markets are bad.

99

New Five-Year Rules for Reopening Returns

Canadians always make mistakes and miss items that could save them tax when they complete their tax returns. It's to be expected. After all, we are only human aren't we? And, the tax return itself seems to get more and more complicated every year. As it stands now we are allowed to go back and reopen three years' worth of tax returns if we find we have missed something or made a mistake. Under new legislation we are going to be able to go back and reopen an extra two years' worth of returns. That means taxpayers will be able to retrieve an extra two years' worth of taxes plus interest in some cases.

In addition to getting back money that is ours, we should also act as soon as possible as we could earn a bonus. Until the legislation is passed we can't expect to reclaim this money. And when it is it will still take a long time to get a response as this will be in addition to the yearly chore of checking 17 million tax returns and all the assessments that are done as the year progresses.

Revenue Canada sources tell me that if you discover a mistake you should write Revenue Canada. Include your name, address, social insurance number and a description of your problem. When the legislation passes and they can start looking at these cases they will pay you interest retroactive to the date of your letter if you are proven correct.

After the legislation is passed into law the same problem will exist, that is, having enough staff to handle the workload. It might be months or years before you get your money. Interest will apply as of the time you sent the letter. All the more reason why you want to look back at those old tax returns right away. If you find something questionable take the time to write the letter. It might pay off double.

I always recommend that taxpayers remember their old tax returns when they are doing this yearly chore. When you learn a new strategy think of whether it could have been used in past years. You might save taxes this year and in the past.

100

If You Really Want to Earn Interest, Try This Tax-Saving Idea

Tax-free income's a lot better than taxable income in my view. Naturally, the yield is important too, but that's why we always compare after-tax yields to see which investment is better for us.

Term deposits and Canada Savings Bonds normally pay set rates of return. The stock markets and other volatile investments don't always guarantee any rate of return but they may pay off many times over when you hit them right.

There is a combination of the two, though, that may be attractive for some investors. There are bonds traded by stock brokers that pay less than the going rate and as a result trade at a discount to the market. In very simple terms, that means that you earn something like the savings account rate but you only have to pay a portion of the face value of the bond. However, when that bond matures one or more years down the road, you are guaranteed to receive the full face value of the bond.

You paid 80 cents on the dollar, let's say, but you get back 100 cents on the dollar, plus you've been earning interest as long as you held the bond.

The advantage, of course, is that the 20 cents on the dollar increase is treated as a capital gain — as long as you don't exceed $100,000 in your lifetime. It's a nice way to combine the safety of bonds with some capital gains advantages. By the way, don't worry about interest rates rising. You're always guaranteed the face value on the maturity date.

101

If You Don't Need the Regular Income, Don't Take It

Too often our desire for a physical display of success costs us tax dollars.

Canadians are notorious for earning interest income. We like to buy things like term deposits, guaranteed investment certificates and Canada Savings Bonds because they produce a regular income. But don't forget that all interest is taxable. That's why it's better to seek out dividends or capital gains. We can earn as much as $22,000 a year in tax-free Canadian dividends and up to $100,000 in tax-free capital gains. Knowing this, those Canadians who earn interest should look at switching to Canadian dividend-paying stocks or mutual funds to produce tax-free dividend income. Or they should give some serious thought to buying things that will appreciate in value.

A principal residence is a classic choice. If you rent you pay for the property for the landlord. If you buy your own house you have to commit yourself to monthly mortgage payments, utilities and maintenance. However, you at least know that the property will rise in value tax free in your own name.

Rather than having to claim the interest as taxable income each year, you'll own investments that will rise in value tax free as long as you own them. When you sell them there may be a tax problem, but that's only *if* you sell them.

102

If You Rally Want to Save Tax, Don't Earn Interest Income

One reason why so many Canadians pay more tax than necessary is that they choose to earn too much interest income. They like the idea of having a regular income every year or the ability to see their yield, then compound it.

The problem, though, is that when we earn interest that interest is taxable, either every year or at least every three years. However, if we buy assets that produce no income, but instead simply rise in value, we'll never have to pay tax until we sell the investment. Then we'll trigger a capital gain.

For example: If we buy a piece of raw land, that land will rise in value completely tax free until we sell it. We don't have to pay any tax each year or every three years. All our money compounds until we sell. In fact, the same theory applies to art, antiques, real estate, stocks and mutual funds. They can all rise in value completely tax free until they are sold.

Under present legislation we may not even have to pay tax when we sell these investments. The first $100,000 worth of capital gains is tax free. That means we subtract our purchase price from the price we receive when we sell and the first $100,000 is tax free. When we calculate the purchase price it's important that we add on any costs to complete the transaction, such as commissions. And, when we calculate the selling price it's important we consider only the net, in-pocket, after-expense proceeds.

In addition, don't forget that when we invest in small businesses and operating farms that as much as $500,000 in capital gains can be tax free. As a result, picking the right investment can produce substantially more tax-free income than normal.

Once we exceed the $100,000 or $500,000 limits we can still prosper by choosing investments that rise in value rather than produce a regular income. Under existing legislation no more than 75% of capital gains can be considered taxable income. Once we become taxable, 100% of salary attracts tax. When we earn interest income it is totally taxable and even dividends must be added to our income before we get to use the dividend tax credit. When it comes to capital gains at least one-quarter will be tax free with only three-quarters taxable. As a result, capital gains remain one of the lowest-taxed types of income we can earn.

103

Swapping Dividends Can Save Taxes

There's a substantial advantage to earning dividends from Canadian companies. The dividend tax credit wipes out most of the tax bill. In fact, for many taxpayers it allows them to earn up to $22,000 in tax-free investment income.

The problem, though, is that the dividend tax credit isn't a tax deduction. It's a rebate of taxes that you've already paid for a waiving of taxes that you were going to pay. But if you don't owe any taxes, how can you use a credit? And, if you didn't pay any taxes, how can you get them back?

Well, that's the dilemma that some taxpayers face. They may not have enough income to be able to fully use the dividend tax credit. In that case, they have two choices. One is to sell the stocks and buy term-deposit-type investments. The other — and the better choice in my mind — is to look at transferring your dividends and the dividend tax credit to your spouse's tax return.

If your spouse would have been able to claim you as a dependant had you not received these dividends, you have that option. Your spouse would now be able to claim you as a dependant exemption and will be able to use the dividend tax credit to wipe out tax on his or her tax return.

Make sure you do all the paperwork, though, as you don't always win by making this switch.

And make sure you transfer all the Canadian dividends. When you use this option you have to transfer them all, or none at all.

104

Limited Partnerships Limit Liability but Maximize Tax Savings

If you want sizable tax savings, give some thought to one of the more sophisticated tax shelters. Generally, they're only for the higher income groups but there are occasions when they can help others as well.

A limited partnership is a share of an ongoing business. Normally, it's one that's just starting, but there are occasions when an existing business may be syndicated in a limited partnership format.

The advantages? Well, that's an easy one. You get extra-large tax deductions in the early years. Let's say this tax shelter is a hotel that's presently under construction. The investor buys shares in this development well before the construction is completed. That means there's little chance to generate any income for the couple of years in which the building is under construction. At the same time the business is in the process of building this hotel it's going to incur some sizable expenses: interest on borrowed money, operating expenses, depreciation. All of these expenses can be passed through to the investor. Those expenses can be used to lower tax on any forms of income the investor earns. That saves substantial tax dollars in the early years.

Once the building is completed, it's hoped that it will be profitable and produce positive investment income. And the taxman has paid for much of the cost of this investment.

105

Limited Partnerships Can Help Get Money Out of an RRSP Tax Free

While we normally think of a limited-partnership-type tax shelter as most useful for high-income groups, it can be very useful in other special cases.

One example occurs when an individual in the middle-income bracket wants to remove a chunk of money from an RRSP. We know that money removed from an RRSP must be added to our income and taxed at our marginal tax rate (the highest level we qualify for). As a result, we may not want to remove this money. However, if we could create a tax deduction that would offset the money coming out of our RRSP we'd effectively eliminate the tax bill.

One recent limited partnership vehicle comes to mind. It produced a $28,000 tax deduction in the first year. As a result, the investor would be able to remove $28,000 from his or her RRSP without paying any tax on it. In the first five years, in fact, there was enough offsetting tax relief that the investor would be able to remove $87,000 from an RRSP totally tax free.

In doing so the money would not only come out tax free but would be used to pay for shares in an ongoing limited partnership which would eventually provide a decent rate of return as long as the investor continued to own it.

In addition, once the business is doing well share values should rise. Selling them would create a capital gain that could be within the tax-free limit.

What you've accomplished, then, is to save a chunk of taxes on your RRSP withdrawal and use them to buy what could be a tax-free capital gain.

106

Diversify for High Returns

Do you diversify when you invest your money? No, I'm not really referring to spreading your money among a number of different deposit-taking institutions. I'm talking about spreading your money around a number of different products. I think it's a serious mistake when we put everything we have in the same type of investment.

Consider this example. Turn the clock back 20 years. Throughout the last 20 years the average term deposit has paid an average annual rate of return of slightly less than 10%. If we compounded $10,000 at 10% a year for the last 20 years we would have a grand total of $67,274 before tax and, of course, inflation. Unfortunately, taxes would take a substantial bite out of this total.

If, instead, you decided to diversify let's see how well you would have done. Let's say you took $2,000 and bought some highly speculative investment, so speculative, in fact, that you lost everything. Not only did you earn nothing over 20 years you lost the original $2,000, so you would have a zero percent yield.

If you took another $2,000 and left it in a savings account that earned five percent for 20 years, you'd have a total of $5,306.

If you put the next $2,000 in a typical term deposit that was fully covered by deposit insurance and earned 10% a year, you'd have another $13,455.

Let's say you put another $2,000 into a stock portfolio or some very conservative mutual funds that paid a combination of dividends and capital gains that compounded at 15% a year. You'd have a total of $32,733 after 20 years.

Finally, if you took another $2,000 and put it into one of the top-quality mutual funds you'd have another $54,786. In this example I've used an annual compound rate of 18%. The top-quality mutual funds with good management can generally be counted on to earn 16% to 18% to 20% a year averaged over this period of time. Granted, last year is a perfect example of the rationale that performance must be seen as an average. Some years will be bad, others will more than make up for them.

The top-quality mutual funds in this country, as far as I am concerned, include names like Mackenzie Financial, the United Group of Funds, Trimark, Bolton Tremblay, 20/20, AGF, Universal, Templeton and a handful of others. The 18% yield I have used in the last example is the 20-year performance record documented by Templeton Growth Fund.

If we total the amount of money accumulated in each of the five investments outlined above we have a total of $106,280 after 20 years. By going with a single term deposit of $10,000 we would have accumulated only $67,274. The shortfall is $39,006 over 20 years or $1,950.30 a year. In the simplest of terms it cost us almost 20% a year of our original investment because we stuck with one investment rather than diversifying.

Now, these numbers are based on past performance. It's easy to document and prove what has happened in the past. It's more difficult to predict what will happen in the future. However, there's a strong belief that interest rates will stay low for a number of years. Central banks around the world are doing their best to squeeze inflation out of our system. Michael Wilson, our past finance minister, and Mr. Crow, the governor of the Bank of Canada, have announced their beliefs that Canadian inflation will fall 1% to 2% a year in coming years. Even if they are only half-right interest rates will fall further and stay low for some period of time. As a result, I feel it will be difficult to average 10% a year in term deposits over the next 20 years. Even if interest rates rise substantially in coming years the starting point is extremely important. If you earn a high yield in an early year you will compound a larger amount for the rest of the term. But, right now we are going to earn a low rate in the early years.

I have no idea what rate of return we will earn in the stock markets, real estate and mutual funds in coming years. However, if interest rates are going to be low history says this type of investment will do better than normal. As a result, I suspect that we will average at least as much as we did over the past 20 years. But, don't forget that the 10% or so average over the past 20 years for term deposits includes some hefty returns in the late 1970s and early 1980s when interest rates reached 20% and more per year. It's highly unlikely Central Bankers will ever let that happen again.

Even then, the key is to not put all our eggs in one basket. Why not spread our money around. Keep some in term deposits and GICs and Canada Savings Bonds where you have the ultimate in security. But, put some of your money in stocks, mutual funds and real estate as well. Even with the odd dud you will still come out ahead.

107

How To Declare Capital Gains to Your Best Advantage

Sometimes I hear people say, "Why should I bother to declare any capital gains I earned? I mean, they're tax free so why go through the paperwork of declaring them on my tax return?" The thinking is right, I guess, in that all we are really doing when we declare our gains is doing the paperwork for Revenue Canada. We must declare our capital gains on page 1 of our tax returns and then remove them on page 2. As a result, they end up being tax free until we exceed $100,000 worth of normal capital gains or $500,000 worth of capital gains created by selling a farm. On our 1991 tax return (to be filed early in 1992) we will also be able to claim up to $500,000 in tax-free gains from selling a small business.

The real reason why we *must* declare our capital gains is to help Revenue Canada know when we exceed our tax-free limits. Many think they'll never by so lucky. But you'd be surprised how quickly you can get there. A couple of real estate transactions, a killing in the stock markets or mutual funds and you're there. And Revenue Canada wants its share as soon as we pass the tax-free limits.

Revenue Canada can also use this information to tax us earlier than normal. For example, if you created your capital gains in the wrong order you could pay dearly. The first $100,000 worth of gains we report will be credited toward the $100,000 of ordinary tax-free capital gains, no matter how they were earned. That means that selling a farm that created $100,000 worth of capital gains would create a tax-free gain, but we wouldn't be able to earn any other tax-free capital gains. If you were in this position you could benefit by selling all your stocks and mutual funds before closing your farm deal. The stock or mutual-fund gains would be tax free as ordinary gains and the farm gains would be tax free as part of the remaining $400,000 of farm or small-business capital gains. When we declare our gains we have to declare the date of the transaction, which will give Revenue Canada the ability to cross-reference our gains and maybe levy extra tax.

When we declare a stock-market or mutual-fund gain we give the purchase price and sale price. As a result, it's pretty easy to cross-reference these items. When it comes to real estate, though, it's not quite as easy. If the property has been owned for a long time it may be difficult to justify the original value for tax purposes. And, there are cases where Revenue Canada feels the property was sold for less than market value. As a result, they may reassess the capital gain declared.

Why would somebody sell at less than market value? Well, there may have been several properties involved, one of them a tax-free principal residence the value of which was inflated so the taxable property could be reported as generating a small gain.

Another more costly revelation could be the reassessment of capital gains as normal income and, as a result, fully taxable income. An individual who actively buys and sells real estate can be considered a professional. They may buy a property, renovate it and sell it at a nice profit. The profit was created, though, by the renovation. Revenue Canada, in many cases, will consider this as earned income similar to a salary. As a result, it will be fully taxable. Revenue Canada will definitely be looking for taxpayers who report a number of different transactions on their tax returns.

There are other reasons why Revenue Canada wants us to report our capital gains that may not seem as important, but can whittle away at our take-home paycheques. While capital gains can be tax free they can also trigger the alternative minimum tax. As a result, part of our gains could become taxable. While being able to claim the capital-gains deduction on page 2 of our returns appears to make capital gains tax free, the inclusion of the income can eliminate other tax benefits. The net income line determines whether we can claim a relative as a dependant exemption. If that relative claimed capital gains he or she could be eroded or eliminated as a tax exemption. In addition, it's our net income that determines whether or not we can claim the child tax credit or the federal sales tax credit. Claiming capital gains once again could cost us taxes indirectly.

It would be so much easier if we didn't have to claim our capital gains until we exceeded the tax-free levels. However, it's obvious why Revenue Canada wants us to claim them each year. We do their paperwork for them and they stand to gain revenue in other ways.

By the way, if you think it's not worth doing the paperwork consider this. If Revenue Canada finds that we didn't declare our tax-free capital gains they have the power to deny us the entire tax-free capital gains limits.

108

Don't Forget to Claim Capital Losses

For some reason taxpayers have come to believe that capital losses are no longer tax deductible. I guess it has to do with tax-free capital gains. Once we were offered one-half-million dollars in tax-free capital gains we were led to believe that losses were no longer useful. However, now that the half-million has been slashed to $100,000, except for operating farms and small businesses, we should give very serious thought to calculating capital losses. They can be very helpful in extending the tax-free capital gains limit well past the advertised levels.

Here's what I mean. If you earn $100,000 in capital gains you don't have to worry about normal income taxes. I say normal as capital gains in this example are free of ordinary income taxes. However, there is something called the alternative minimum tax that can indeed create a tax problem when you earn large capital gains on top of your other income. If the amounts are small, by the way, you probably don't have to worry about the AMT.

The next problem is when you earn more than $100,000 in capital gains. Then you have to pay tax on two-thirds to three-quarters of the gain at your normal tax rate. In that case it's easy to understand the value of capital losses. All you have to do is sell your losers to manufacture losses that offset your gains.

Now, in some cases that might seem unreasonable in that these clunkers may, if only in your own mind, have the potential to make you a millionaire sometime in the future. You bought them to make money. Why would you want to dump them before you did? Well, don't worry. We can manufacture some tax relief and still own these future winners. All you have to do is sell them at a loss and buy them back again later. Now, their new purchase price, while the same as the selling price, is lower than the original purchase price. When they do rise in value you'll have to claim the gains as capital gains. But that will be some time in the future and you've already used the losses to save taxes by offsetting capital gains. In addition, we can always hope that by that time there will be new rules that will make these capital gains tax free or at least taxed at a lower rate.

Most people feel they will never make it to $100,000 or $500,000 in capital gains. But, who knows? You could always win the lottery and be loaded with investable cash. Or, all you need is a good long-term purchase program and your money will be constantly in place to produce profits. And, what if you inherit some money or the family cottage? Believe me it doesn't take long to produce enough capital gains to be taxable either as a taxable capital gain or as part of the alternative minimum tax.

For example, what if you have a $20,000 capital gain, Yes, you may not feel it is taxable but you still have to claim it on your tax return as a gain. That may affect other tax calculations or the AMT. If, at the same time, you could trigger $10,000 in capital losses you could lower your real capital gains to only $10,000. That might help you tax-wise.

You may also want to think ahead. Under tax reform the amount of our capital gains that must be used in our calculations gradually escalated from 50% to 66.33% to 75%. If you fear that the percentages may rise you may want to trigger capital gains and losses sooner. If you feel that the percentage of taxable gains will fall you have more incentive to trigger capital losses now to offset your capital gains.

It's also imperative that you look to the future when you consider capital losses. We've gone through a very confusing period to tax changes. Who knows how long we'll even be able to claim any tax-free capital gains or be able to offset our taxable gains with capital losses? If you have even the slightest fear I'd always trigger capital gains when the investment merited it and capital losses when it was best.

109

When You Earn a Tax-Free Capital Gain, You Can Also Earn Other Income

While earning a pure capital gain will save taxes, it doesn't produce much of a yearly income. That's why it's generally better to combine capital gains with other investments.

For example: rental real estate. If you buy a duplex or triplex, you'll own an investment that can rise in value totally free of tax. In addition, though, you'll have somebody paying part of the cost of owning this property — the tenants.

There are other examples to consider as well — a mutual fund, for one. When you buy a mutual fund you group your money together with that of other investors. The portfolio manager then has enough money to buy and sell shares in a large group of companies rather than limiting your exposure to only a few. If the fund earns a capital gain it will pass it on to the investors. In addition, the fund may own shares that produce dividends. Those dividends can be passed on to the investors as well. If they're Canadian, they will qualify for the dividend tax credit that allows many Canadians to earn as much as $22,000 a year in tax-free dividends. In addition, the mutual fund may also produce interest income and if the value of the units themselves rises, they also can be sold at a capital gain. In effect, then, you end up with a double chance for a tax-free capital gain plus virtually tax-free dividends plus some interest. But at least the interest is kept to a minimum.

Another example is a stock portfolio. If you buy good quality stocks with a good record of paying dividends, you'll be in position to earn a tax-free capital gain at the same time as you receive dividend income.

One major advantage to this type of investing is that you have income coming in to help you survive the downturns in the markets. In addition, because you have both a regular income and the prospects of a future profit, Revenue Canada is prepared to let you claim interest on loans taken to help you buy these investments as a tax deduction.

110

An Illness, as Sad as It May Be, May Save Taxes

Medical expenses are tax deductible but only when handled properly. The first consideration is that there's no longer an automatic 3% of net-income threshold level. Before tax reform we could only claim our medical expenses as tax deductions when they exceeded 3% of our net income. As a result, the higher your income the tougher it was to create any tax deductions through claiming medical expenses. Under tax reform it appeared at first that it was going to be even more difficult to claim medical expenses because our net incomes were going to rise as some tax deductions that previously came before the net-income line were shifted to later positions in the tax return. However, Revenue Canada has included an "either/or" offer. We can use the lesser of 3% of our net income or $1,500 when calculating our medical expenses. As a result, it's generally easier to claim medical expenses in the name of the spouse who earns less than $50,000 in net income. They will be able to claim their medical expenses faster as their threshold level will be less than $1,500.

In Revenue Canada's eyes husband and wife are one when it comes to medical expenses. As a result spouses can combine their medical expenses at tax time. If there are children involved, though, they cannot automatically be included. The only way a child's medical expenses can be claimed by a parent is to claim the child as a dependant tax credit on that parent's tax return. And, under tax reform Revenue Canada generally expects the higher-income spouse to claim the children as tax credits.

As a result, this year families are going to have to do a little extra tax planning when it comes to claiming medical expenses.

For two-income families where no children are involved it's still worthwhile to try to claim the medical expenses in the lower-income spouse's name. Approximately 26% of these medical expenses will be treated as a tax credit no matter which spouse's name is used. However, by claiming in the lower-income spouse's name the medical expenses will be tax deductible sooner provided the lower-income spouse's net income is lower than $50,000.

When children are involved it is beneficial to attempt to claim the child who experienced these medical expenses as a dependant of the parent who will benefit most when it comes time to claim the family medical expenses. As a result, they will become tax deductible sooner. However, it should be remembered that the taxman wants us to claim the family allowance cheque in the name of the higher-income spouse.

It's also possible to juggle medical expenses incurred in different years on to one tax return. While we normally think of medical expenses on a year-to-year basis there is an advantage to overlapping back-to-back years. You see, Revenue Canada allows us to claim medical expenses in a yearly or 12-month period as long as the 12 months end in the taxation year. That means that an individual or family that incurred some substantial medical expenses in overlapping years may be able to lump those expenses into one tax year.

Here's what you want to do. Look at your medical bills over the past year. If you find that they generally occur on a month-to-month basis you will probably want to stick with the normal yearly calculation. However, if you find that you incurred some substantial medical expenses partway through the year you should consider claiming on a 12-month period rather than on a calendar-year basis.

The problem with the calendar-year basis is that each year you must exceed $1,500 or an amount equal to 3% of your net income in expenses before you can claim any medical bills as a tax deduction. If you were able to merge your medical bills from the last half of one year and the first half of the next, let's say, you would be able to claim the bulk of two years' worth of expenses with only one threshold level. For example, if you had $1,500 a year in medical expenses you may get no tax relief because of the threshold level. However, if you could lump those bills together you would be able to claim $3,000 worth of medical bills in one year. The first $1,500 wouldn't be tax deductible but the second $1,500 would be.

Using this theory you'll find it beneficial to keep a running total of your medical bills. At certain times you'll find it's beneficial to have elective medical work done. You may have dental work done because it is now tax deductible or get new eyeglasses or have other work done because the taxman will pick up part of the cost.

111

Win a Lottery? Take the Money Properly

Few people win the lottery, even the small prizes. But if you're lucky enough to hold a big winning ticket, make sure you take the prize properly.

Sometimes individuals share tickets so they have a number of prize-winning opportunities. In that case the prizes are legitimately split between the subscribing partners. In other cases families will buy tickets between themselves with the prizes being split based on the amount contributed by each spouse. In the case of a husband and wife — or children for that matter — this opens the door to some possible tax savings.

Let's say you win a large prize — say $100,000 or so. Normally a husband and wife would split it down the middle. In fact, property rights suggest they wouldn't have much choice. But upon assessing a family's financial situation you might find it better to have one spouse collect all the money.

One circumstance would be when one spouse already has most of the family's assets in his or her name. There are many families where only one spouse has worked. As a result, the pension, the RRSPs, the investments, etc., are all lumped in one spouse's name. What better chance to legitimately accumulate a chunk of money in the other spouse's name. Most of the winnings will be invested, so if the money is split evenly, the working spouse will see his or her tax bill rise. If the money is aimed at the lower-income spouse, any investment earnings will be taxed at a lower rate. So make sure you accept lottery winnings properly.

112

When Santa Has Financial Smarts

So, here it is almost Christmas time and you're struggling to find those last-minute gifts that you need. Well, why not think financial? No, not cost — make the theme something that will eventually create wealth, large or small, for the recipient.

For example, have you considered giving a subscription to one of the excellent money-type magazines that are available? *Financial Post Moneywise Magazine*, *Canadian Business* and *Venture* are several that come to mind that offer excellent, down-to-earth, money-saving ideas for most sectors of the population.

Or, what about a subscription to a newspaper with a good business section? It could be your local newspaper, a regional one, or a totally business-oriented publication like *The Financial Post* or *Financial Times*. The recipient may actually find enough investment tips and tax-saving ideas that the subscription price will be saved many times over. In addition, there are several more in-depth publications that could prove valuable. *The Wall Street Journal* is one that come to mind.

Another choice is a subscription to one of the monthly newsletters that have become so popular in the last few years. The advantage here, of course, is that you can pick one that zeroes in on the area of expertise that most appeals to your recipient. You can pick financial planning, the stock market, real estate, international finance — almost anything you want.

If you're not excited by any of these financial ideas you might go further and offer the real thing — a paid-for session with a financial consultant. The cost will vary with the length of the meeting so make sure you determine how long it will last. Here, though, you have even more flexibility in that you can pick a financial planner who is involved in a specific area.

Business-type books have been amongst the most popular in recent years. And this year is no exception with a long list of new editions. There are books on small business, the future of the economy, stock markets, mutual funds and personal financial planning. Personally, I prefer the latter — not because it's my type of writing, but because they help individuals learn to manage their own money. That will save them money and taxes in future years. As a result, a gift like this could be used and remembered for many years in the future.

What about giving a specific investment? Canada Savings Bonds would appear to be the natural as they can be purchased in small amounts and are virtually risk free. Unfortunately, though, they require some foresight as they are only on sale in the fall. You might want to consider some CSBs as gifts next fall — well in advance of the Christmas season.

More sophisticated investments could also prove valuable as Christmas gifts, especially for children, as they may encourage them to think financially well ahead of schedule. Mutual funds and stocks may not sound terribly attractive after a stock market sell-off. However, history has proven that the best managed, the conservative, the blue chip stocks and mutual funds will outperform most other investments over a reasonable period of time. Funds like Templeton Growth, Industrial Growth, United Funds, Cundill Value, Trimark and other well-established funds historically yield 15% and 25% per year. The younger the person you give them to, the greater the likelihood the funds will pay off.

The same theory applies to stocks. Buy something that has long-term potential. In fact, that might be the perfect gift for a youngster — some shares in a small company that might explode to be worth a ton of money down the road. An example would be Soft Key, an exciting software company listed on the Toronto Stock Exchange, and NASDAQ in New York. This company is a master in marketing software in North America. Analysts look for big things from them in the future as computers continue to take over our lives.

For children, there's an especially attractive stock issue. They like toys. They break toys. Why not give them shares of a toy company like Irwin Toy? They profit as toy sales improve, and they also get to join Irwin's junior shareholders club. Once members, they are invited to the annual meeting where they get a preview of all the new toys for the coming year and even get one to take home as an extra dividend.

And don't forget gold and other precious metals. Coins and gold wafers are especially interesting in that they can be converted into jewelry that may well rise in value in future years — a gift that appreciates in value, not one that is soon forgotten.

113

What Does the Future Hold for Tax Rates?

"Why bother contributing to an RRSP when I'll only pay more tax when I remove the money than I saved when I contributed it? After all, tax rates have a habit of rising over time — and if I'm any good my salary will rise in future years." That's the question I received in a recent letter.

Quite frankly, this writer isn't the only taxpayer who feels this way. And I suppose there may be a few who actually will fall into this position. But, for most taxpayers the opposite is the case — they will pay lower tax rates when they remove the money from their RRSPs than they saved when they originally made the contributions.

In addition, don't forget that the tax-free compounding available inside an RRSP will give you much more money down the road. Even if the tax rates were higher, the much bigger pot of money will produce more after-tax income.

The real question is this — will tax rates be higher in coming years?

We know the federal government is committed to lowering marginal tax brackets. First we had tax reform, then the introduction of the GST. It's highly likely that in coming years the GST rate will be increased with offsetting reductions in the marginal tax brackets. Elections, of course, can always have an impact.

Recognizing that eventuality, we can do some future planning. The maximum tax rate in 1987 was around 53%. For 1988 it fell to the 44% to 46% range. Moving money from 1987 to 1988, then, was an attractive tax planning tactic. However, the same theories can provide even more benefit over the long term.

Check the tax rates in some of the American states. In Florida and many other states the maximum federal and state tax bill is

28%. That's so much lower than Canadian rates that Ottawa can't help but worry that Canadians will hide money in the American states where tax rates are that low. In fact, the classic case has self-employed, small-business types buying the goods that they sell through an American company that they own. They simply mark up the price they pay so there's little profit recorded in Canada and all kinds of profits reported in the U.S. where tax bills are lower. Their expenses will, naturally, be reported in Canada where the tax relief would produce the biggest savings.

Ottawa recognizes this can and will happen. As a result, they know they must lower our taxes further. At the same time they know they can't lower our tax bills because they still have a substantial budget deficit. That's where the changes in sales taxes hit us. They plan to increase sales-tax rates at the same time as they reduce marginal tax rates. It will take some time but I think our maximum marginal tax rates can fall to the 36% range in another four or five years.

Given that, there's no question that we should clearly take every tax deduction we can find right now so we will save taxes at today's tax rates. If we leave the money inside our RRSP for four or five years we should be able to remove it at a much lower tax rate.

In past years there's no question that saving taxes then didn't guarantee that we'd repay them at a lower rate down the road. Yes, the faster compounding inside a tax-free environment made an RRSP very attractive. Now, though, the virtual guarantee that tax rates will fall in coming years makes an RRSP a four- to five-year plan, not a lifetime program. Naturally, it's also better to look much further down the road. Beginning this year, all interest is fully taxable. That means long-term compounding is very valuable. If you can put your money into a long-term investment you will be able to compound both your principal and interest plus the normal share of the interest that would have gone to the taxman. As a result you have much more to work with down the road.

Sure, it's easy to say that registered retirement savings plans are valuable as short-term tax-saving devices, but the real value is long-term compounding. The tax rebates gained can be used for whatever purpose you choose while the money inside can be compounded for as long as you wish, rather than only three years outside the plan.

The key is don't ignore these plans because you aren't interested in long-term investments. Take the tax relief first. In almost all cases the money can be removed at a lower tax rate. It just takes a little planning.

114

Page One of Your Tax Return: A Checkup for This Year

Do you know the biggest problem with our tax system? No, it's not the complexity, although that is a major problem. No, it's not the high percentage of our incomes that we pay in taxes because there are things we can do to avoid many of these taxes. It's the way we use the tax system, the way we refuse to do things that could help us.

This is tax time. Most of us fear the tax return. However, what we should really be doing is using it to our advantage. We should use it as a yearly checkup of our financial health. I mean it stands to reason that those who have a medical checkup each year will find things that are wrong before they become more serious problems. The same works with our tax returns. We have to file one each year so why not use the information we find to help us rearrange our finances so we don't have problems in future years.

Do you do your own tax return or do you have somebody else prepare it? I find that many of the taxpayers who do it themselves simply get out last year's tax return and fill in the same areas. Things they missed in past years get passed by again this year. If somebody else checked your tax return you may have found things that you should have used in past years that you can still use, as tax returns can be reopened for three years and under new legislation, we may be able to go back five years.

Many taxpayers who pay a service to complete their tax returns do no more than sign the back of the return and mail it in. Take the time to go over the return with a financial planner to ensure that everything possible was done and to ensure that you understand the value of changing strategies.

One thing a financial planner may notice might include line 115, Other Pensions. If you claim any income on this line you may be entitled to claim the Pension Income deduction on line 314. Social pensions do not qualify. However, you can manufacture your own pension if you don't presently receive one. You could even cash in some investments that are presently producing taxable interest and replace them with the equivalent of $1,000 in tax-free pension income.

If you use line 101 you are a typical employee. However, if you use line 102 you earn commission-type income and are entitled to claim many of your business expenses.

If you have young children you receive the family allowance cheque. There is no way to avoid claiming this income on the higher income spouse's tax return. However, once you use this line a financial planner should trigger you to consider income splitting. That's the practice of putting this money into investments for the children. That way the yield will normally grow tax free rather than produce taxable income in your own name. Those who normally prefer interest income will benefit more from income splitting this way as interest income is taxed at our highest tax rate.

If you claim a reasonable amount of income on line 121 you earn interest income. While it's safe and normally secure it is also taxed heavily. If you wish to lower your tax bill you would be better off switching to dividend-paying stocks or mutual funds. Dividends are claimed one line earlier. While they are still taxable they qualify for the dividend tax credit later in the tax return which can allow many taxpayers to earn as much as $22,000 in tax-free dividend income each year.

If you don't use line 122 it means you have not participated in any limited partnerships in recent years. Included were syndicated investments in town houses, hotels, condominiums, etc. If you didn't participate in the past you may be happy as real estate prices have cooled. However, looking at one now might be a different story. You would manufacture some tax relief for future years while "getting in" in a buyer's market. Always be careful when you invest in this type of project. They can work wonderfully in reducing taxes. However, if the investment is a bust, what does it matter if you got some tax relief.

A financial planner would also look at line 126, Rental Income. It amazes me how often taxpayers report their gross rental income but when they report net rental income it's zero. How can you hit exactly on zero? If you have positive rental income it is added to your other forms of income. If your expenses are greater than your income you have negative rental income. For some reason many people don't realize that negative income can be claimed as a loss. It will automatically reduce the tax you pay on your other forms of income.

Remember, when you get to the bottom of page 1 you have your Total Income. There's nothing you can do about it for 1990. But, using your tax return as a financial checkup can show you how you should be changing your strategies for this year.

115

Page Two of Your Tax Return: A Tool for the Future

When you do your tax return it's a crying shame if you don't use it as a tool to find out where you went wrong, financially speaking, in the past year.

It's too late to save taxes for 1990. We earned what we earned, we used the tax-saving ideas we chose, and now we're stuck with the tax bill we have to pay. However, it's not too late, in fact it's the perfect time, to use the information we used to file this tax return to improve our tax situation in 1991.

In the previous chapter I wrote of the importance of assessing the information reported on page 1 of your return. Our abilities are restricted there as we have few areas with which to work. Page 2 gives us a number of serious alternatives we should consider for future tax-saving advantages.

The first line we can use to our advantage on page 2 is the registered pension plan line. If you can contribute to your pension plan at work it no longer has much impact on your contribution limits to your registered retirement savings plan. We are all entitled to 18% of last year's earned income to a maximum of $11,500 for 1991. From that amount we must subtract the amount we contribute to our pension plan at work or we must subtract our pension adjustment (the amount of benefit our employer tells us we receive from our combined pension contributions). If you have the ability to contribute to your pension plan at work or your RRSP at home you should make a decision right away. If your employer matches your pension contributions you virtually double your money overnight. As a result, it probably pays to contribute to your pension plan at work. You have an extra advantage in that the money is automatically deducted from your paycheque at work so it's easier to save for the future.

If your employer doesn't match your contributions it probably pays to skip line 207 and concentrate on the next line instead.

If you didn't use the maximum allowable limit on line 208 you aren't with it. Registered retirement savings plans are well on their way to being the only tax-saving device we have left. If you didn't use this line to the fullest on this year's tax return you should calculate how much you can contribute for this year. If you make your contribution through a financial planner now you can ask for a tax receipt that can reduce the withholding taxes on your earnings throughout the rest of the year. This year is especially important as this year's RRSP contribution is based on income you already know you earned last year. You already know how much you can contribute so it's a lot easier this year.

Check line 214, Child Care Expenses. If you paid child-care expenses last year but weren't able to claim them maybe you should be looking to rearrange your schedule so you can. In addition, don't forget that you can claim child-care expenses actually paid even though they weren't for a particular child. For example, if you paid more for one child than you can claim but had another child late in the year you can claim costs incurred for both even though they were actually incurred for only the one child.

If you feel you paid too much tax last year but used everything on your form you should pay special attention to the next few lines on the return. Lines 217, 221 and 224 allow you to manufacture tax relief. If you are looking to use them this year it's better to get started early. We used to be able to lump a large number of carrying charges and development expenses together right near the end of the year. Recently, though, the rules have been tightened so that many have to be amortized over a number of years. Getting started early increases the amount we can claim for 1991.

If you want to reduce your taxes you can buy a tax shelter now. Too often we wait until the end of the year when we compete with everybody else for the leftovers. Now is particularly attractive for two reasons. Most of this type of tax shelter involves real estate. Real estate prices are low now thanks to the recession. In addition tax rates have risen to almost unbearable heights. Chosen properly now, a tax shelter can provide tax relief plus a handsome capital gain in future years.

Exploration and development expenses should also be considered long-term planning. These are speculative investments in the natural resource industry that may or may not pay off. As a result, they should be chosen carefully with the help of a professional. It's one thing to manufacture some tax relief but you don't want to lose the money you invested either.

Don't just *do* your tax return. Use it as a tax planning textbook. In fact, get an extra copy of the tax return and pretend you used the lines we mentioned. Then you can see the difference in the bottom line.

116

Year-End Tax Tips:
RRSPs and Pensions

While year-end tax planning has always been a must to ensure that we pay as little tax as possible this year it's more important than usual. We're in a recession, the GST is here, the clawback has passed and the investment markets have been struggling.

The Fraser Institute, a Vancouver-based think tank, estimates the average Canadian pays more than 50% of his or her income to the government. If money is tight because of the recession what better way is there to raise a little extra than to cut back on the 50% or so that we pay the taxman.

Before the year is done it's important that you get out last year's tax return and compare your situation last year to this year. If you are happy with the amount of tax you paid last year then do the same things again. If you aren't happy start looking at the things that are available real fast.

The key line is now the net income line. It's line 236 near the top of page 2 of your return. While taxable income will eventually determine your tax bill the net income line has taken on great importance in recent years. It determines whether or not you can claim your dependants as tax deductions, whether you lose the family allowance benefits or old age security because of the clawback and whether you have to pay back other social benefits. By using the deductions that come before the net income line you can save taxes *and* avoid being clawed back on your social benefits.

The first line in the net income section is a deduction for contributing to your pension plan at work. Sadly, many taxpayers wait until the new year to compare whether they should contribute to their pension at work or their registered retirement savings plan at home. You see, any contributions to your pension plan must be in by midnight December 31 each year if you wish to use them as a tax deduction on that year's tax return. Yet, we can wait until the end of February to contribute to an RRSP and still qualify for retroactive tax relief. If you don't make your decision now you may well find out that you should have contributed extra to your pension before year end. Normally, we make this decision by comparing the rates of return we can earn in our pension or RRSP. Because they are more versatile RRSPs generally outperform pensions. However, if you have the right to contribute an extra $1,000, let's say, to your pension at work and your employer matches it you have doubled your money already. Having twice as much money invested easily overcomes a slightly lower yield.

After deciding which plan to use you should use it right away. The sooner the money is in the plan the sooner it starts earning tax-free income inside the plan. If fact, if you can contribute to both your pension and your RRSP you should do it now even though you know you can delay your RRSP contribution until the end of February.

The rules for RRSP contributions for 1991 are as follows. You can contribute up to 18% or your earned income to a maximum of $11,500 if you have no pension at work. If you have a pension it's the same 18% but the maximum is still $11,500. From the $11,500 you must subtract the amount the amount of money you contributed to your pension plan last year, and/or the amount your employer contributed. If you have a defined benefit plan, subtract your pension adjustment (PA). Your PA is found in box 52 of last year's T-4 slip..

One word of caution. The definition of earned income has changed. Basically, it's your earnings from work, plus alimony or maintenance received plus rental real estate income after deducting operating expenses. Pension income no longer qualifies. As a result many pensioners will find their taxable income much higher this year than in the past. As the RRSP is the only deduction that can be manufactured after year end it's imperative that seniors assess their situations immediately to see if there isn't something else they can do.

Some seniors can contribute pension income to a spousal RRSP. If you receive company pension (no social pensions qualify) you can contribute any amount you can afford to a maximum of $6,000 a year to a spousal RRSP provided your spouse hasn't reached age 72. If you don't have the cash to do this you might want to consider removing $6,000 from your RRSP and then contributing it to a spousal RRSP. It won't help your tax situation but it will improve your spouse's opportunity to earn income in future years. It can be used to buy a pension which will be taxed at your spouse's tax rate. If it's lower than yours, you, as a family, are winners.

This strategy only works with married pensioners. And, no, $6,000 or even $12,000 in tax deductions isn't enough to justify marriage. However, if you were thinking about marrying anyway an extra $12,000 in tax deductions may help you make the decision before year end.

117

Year-End Tax Tips: Your Investments

As the year comes to an end it's easy to understand why you should contribute to your pension or registered retirement savings plan. You will save taxes before the year-end deadline. But, what about removing money from a pension, deferred profit-sharing plan or registered retirement savings plan? This may be the natural time for some taxpayers to get their hands on some money at a low tax rate.

We know the unemployment numbers are rising so some taxpayers are going to see some violent swings in their tax rates. If you have already been out of work for some months but expect to return to work full time next year you may want to attack your RRSP and remove some funds. They may be taxed at a low rate. RRSPs are the most flexible but deferred profit savings plans may allow better access. And, pensions, while normally hard to access may also allow some removals. If you were prematurely retired you may have received a golden handshake. Those funds should be rolled into your RRSP so they are not taxable. You could remove some of those funds before year end and pay a lower tax rate than if you worked a full year. If you were let go your company may have returned to you the contributions you made to your company pension plan. If they are not vested you may be able to transfer them to your RRSP and then remove some before year end.

Conversely, if you have worked the entire year but know you are going to be laid off in the new year you should contribute the absolute maximum possible to your RRSP right now even if you don't have the money. You will get a tax deduction at this year's high tax rate but will be able to remove the money early in the new year at next year's expected lower tax rate.

This is also the time of year when you have to decide what to do with your investment portfolios. Stock market and real estate investments are down this year. If you are in position to trigger some losses you might want to, especially when you consider the damaging impact of the new clawback rules. If your net income exceeds $50,850 you will start to lose the family allowance and old age security. If you have already earned some capital gains this year they are tax free until you exceed your $100,000 lifetime tax-free limit. However, when you put them on your tax return they appear on page 1. When you claim the tax-free capital gains deduction it comes on page 2, after the net income line. It's the net income line that will determine whether your family allowance and old age security are clawed back. As a result, you should assess your situation and determine whether or not to trigger some capital losses before the end of the year. Capital losses are not tax deductible against other income. However, if you have earned some gains this year any losses you now trigger would wipe out an equivalent amount of gains *before* they had to be reported on page 1 of your return. That would lower your net income, which could in turn ease the clawback.

Tax loss selling has a deadline. As financial transactions take five days to complete you must trigger these losses at least five days before year end. And, that means five business days. With holidays at this time of year that means you should complete your tax loss selling by December 20 or arrange for your sale to be handled on a cash basis to shorten the normal five-day requirement.

If you have already exceeded your $100,000 in tax-free capital gains you might also consider triggering capital gains before year end. If you feel confident that your tax bracket is going to be higher this year than next you could trigger capital gains now. They would be taxed at a lower rate this year than next. This decision must be made quickly, though, as you must spend some time assessing what your income will be this year and guessing next year's.

This is also the time of year when people load up on tax shelters, say units of a hotel, nursing home, condominium project or self-storage furniture complex. These investments include substantial tax relief, sometimes more than you actually invested, that can be claimed on this year's tax return. A word of caution, though. Don't buy these investments simply for the tax relief. It's great to save taxes. However, if the investment is no good to begin with you will only end up losing more money than you got in tax relief in the first place.

It's best to buy tax shelters from financial planners and stock brokers rather than from the developer. Most developers are reputable but it almost always pays to have an intermediary, somebody who sees many of these investments and has narrowed them down to a select few.

And, don't forget that the longer you wait the fewer choices you will have. The best ones sell out first, the lesser lights will be all that's left at the end of the year.

118

Year-End Tax Tips: Charitable Contributions

We're in a recession, we've set a record for bankruptcies, unemployment rates are rising — and we can get some extra tax relief if we do share with others before the year end.

While Ottawa has been cutting back on the tax deductions we can use to save taxes we do still have the right to claim charitable donations. How we do it can produce extra tax relief.

You must get approved tax receipts. Without them you will be denied deductions. Make sure that one spouse claims all the deductions on his or her tax return. You see, when we contribute to our favorite charities we get a low tax break on the first $250 and substantially more after that.

On the first $250 we save 17% against our federal taxes. When we add on the provincial portion the savings are about 25 cents on the dollar. Once we exceed $250, the savings almost double regardless of our normal tax bracket. Now the federal portion skyrockets to 29%. Adding on the provincial portion means we can save about 45 cents on the dollar. As a result, contributing to charity can save us more tax dollars than any other strategy. High income earners get every tax deduction at their high rate. But lower-income and middle-income types can save a higher than normal amount of taxes by using charitable donations.

Why do I suggest all the charitable contributions go on one spouse's tax return? Well, if we split them each spouse will get a low tax credit on up to $250 each year. If we put them all on one spouse's return we exceed the $250 limit faster. Then, we get much more help from the federal and provincial governments when we help others. Then, we can give more to charities without actually using any more of our own money.

I know that when two spouses each have money they will often want to contribute to the charity of their choice. However, it matters not which spouse's name is on the receipt. They are interchangeable and can be switched from tax return to tax return.

On occasion, you might find both spouses claiming charitable contributions. We are restricted to a maximum of 20% of our net income each year. If you exceed 20% you have two choices. You can transfer some or all of the excess to your spouse's tax return or you can carry the excess over to any of the next five years. Either way, you'll still receive the lower credit against the first $250 so you generally will find you are better off claiming it this year on your spouse's return and getting the tax relief faster.

It's important that you calculate your charitable status before year end. Consider that you donate $250 each year. You always get the low rate. If you gave this year and next year's donations now you'd get almost double the tax relief on the second $250. In fact, people in this situation should always donate double one year and nothing the next. Your charitable donations will cost you less out of pocket so you might be able to give more.

If, by the way, you are prepared to contribute to a government or a government agency you are normally not restricted by the 20% of net income rule.

Don't forget that the net income line is important. Other deductions used before this line can restrict the amount you can contribute each year. Registered retirement savings plans, pension plan contributions, tax shelter deductions, borrowing costs, child-care expenses, moving expenses, alimony and business expenses all come before the net income line. All the more reason why it's so important to calculate your net income before the end of the year, to determine whether to increase your charitable contributions this year or delay a doubling strategy until next.

Many Canadians spend part of the winter in warmer American climes. If you donate to a church or charity in the U.S. you may still be allowed to claim them on your Canadian tax return. If you earn American income, even from investments, or if the charity has received money from the federal government in the past two years you will still be able to claim them.

Printed in Canada